Table of Contents – NDS Game Creation

License Agreement

This book (the "Book") is a product provided by HobbyPRESS (being referred to as "HobbyPRESS" in this document), subject to your compliance with the terms and conditions set forth below. PLEASE READ THIS DOCUMENT CAREFULLY BEFORE ACCESSING OR USING THE BOOK. BY ACCESSING OR USING THE BOOK, YOU AGREE TO BE BOUND BY THE TERMS AND CONDITIONS SET FORTH BELOW. IF YOU DO NOT WISH TO BE BOUND BY THESE TERMS AND CONDITIONS, YOU MAY NOT ACCESS OR USE THE BOOK. HOBBYPRESS MAY MODIFY THIS AGREEMENT AT ANY TIME, AND SUCH MODIFICATIONS SHALL BE EFFECTIVE IMMEDIATELY UPON POSTING OF THE MODIFIED AGREEMENT ON THE CORPORATE SITE OF HOBBYPRESS. YOU AGREE TO REVIEW THE AGREEMENT PERIODICALLY TO BE AWARE OF SUCH MODIFICATIONS AND YOUR CONTINUED ACCESS OR USE OF THE BOOK SHALL BE DEEMED YOUR CONCLUSIVE ACCEPTANCE OF THE MODIFIED AGREEMENT.

Restrictions on Alteration

You may not modify the Book or create any derivative work of the Book or its accompanying documentation. Derivative works include but are not limited to translations.

Restrictions on Copying

You may not copy any part of the Book unless formal written authorization is obtained from us.

LIMITATION OF LIABILITY

HobbyPRESS will not be held liable for any advice or suggestions given in this book. If the reader wants to follow a suggestion, it is at his or her own discretion. Suggestions are only offered to help.

IN NO EVENT WILL HOBBYPRESS BE LIABLE FOR (I) ANY INCIDENTAL, CONSEQUENTIAL, OR INDIRECT DAMAGES (INCLUDING, BUT NOT LIMITED TO, DAMAGES FOR LOSS OF PROFITS, BUSINESS INTERRUPTION, LOSS OF PROGRAMS OR INFORMATION, AND THE LIKE) ARISING OUT OF THE USE OF OR INABILITY TO USE THE BOOK. EVEN IF HOBBYPRESS OR ITS AUTHORIZED REPRESENTATIVES HAVE BEEN ADVISED OF THE POSSIBILITY OF SUCH DAMAGES, OR (II) ANY CLAIM ATTRIBUTABLE TO ERRORS, OMISSIONS, OR OTHER INACCURACIES IN THE BOOK.

You agree to indemnify, defend and hold harmless HobbyPRESS, its officers, directors, employees, agents, licensors, suppliers and any third party information providers to the Book from and against all losses, expenses, damages and costs, including reasonable attorneys' fees, resulting from any violation of this Agreement (including negligent or wrongful conduct) by you or any other person using the Book.

Miscellaneous.

This Agreement shall all be governed and construed in accordance with the laws of Hong Kong applicable to agreements made and to be performed in Hong Kong. You agree that any legal action or proceeding between HobbyPRESS and you for any purpose concerning this Agreement or the parties' obligations hereunder shall be brought exclusively in a court of competent jurisdiction sitting in Hong Kong.

Preface

DS Game Maker had revolutionized the world of NDS 2D game creation, by providing easy visual interface for producing complex game logic, all without writing complex C codes.

The goal of this book is to provide starters with rich technical information so the best decision and judgment can be exercised when creating NDS 2D games through DS Game Maker.

This is not a step-by-step tutorial. This is also not a guide book kind of overview material. We place our focus on the practical side of NDS game creation – practical tips and techniques one will definitely need when starting out a NDS game project. We also tell exactly what can and cannot be done with DS Game Maker, and the kind of performance drawback that can be foreseen when the platform is not fed with the right inputs.

So, are you ready for the challenge?

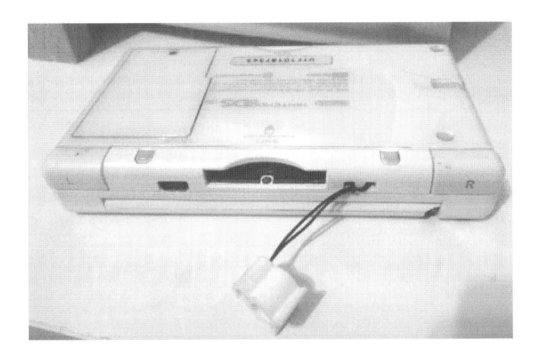

Version Information

Information presented in this book is based on the PRO version.

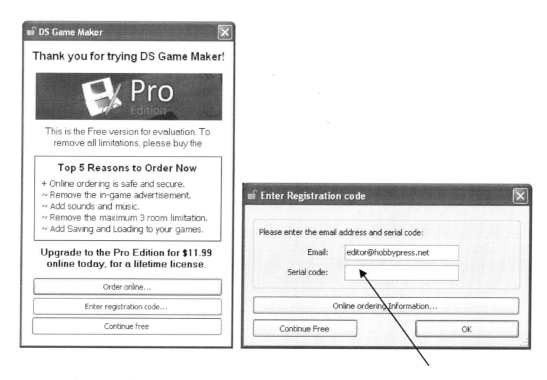

To upgrade to the PRO version, you need to purchase a serial code and activate the software online. To find out the current status of your DS Game Maker installation, click on the upper right icon of the software.

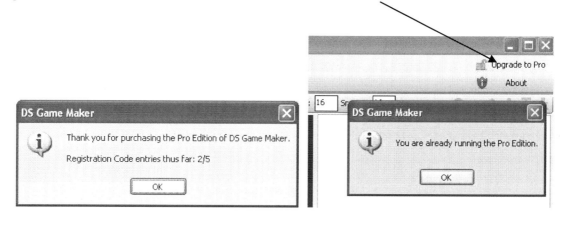

Basic Concepts

What kinds of game is DS Game Maker optimized for? Is

DS Game Maker 3D capable?

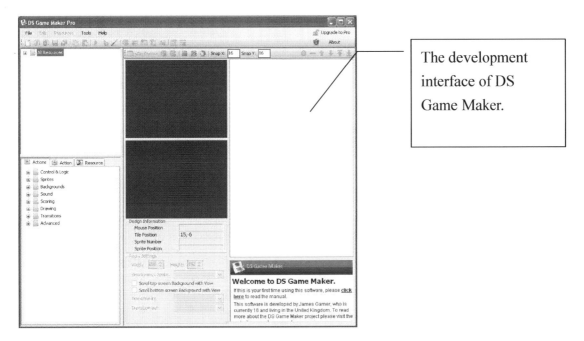

The development interface of DS Game Maker.

DS Game Maker is a development platform that can be used to create a wide range of 2D games on NDS. What this means is that DS Game Maker may simply NOT be optimized for any particular game type. Effective optimization usually requires specialization, but DS Game Maker is more "general-purpose" oriented.

DS Game Maker is primarily a 2D tool, although you can use

3D-like sprites in its 2D view. NDS does have a 3D engine capable of displaying 120,000 polygons per second. This 3D feature, however, is not yet supported by DS Game Maker.

DS Game Maker is NOT a drag and drop tool. It is visual in that it provides a logical layout for different game design elements. However, it does not really allow you to arrange visual elements via mouse drag drop actions.

Why is DS Game Maker a good choice for elementary game

creation?

First of all, good game creation does not have to be 3D capable. Many good games are 2D based.

Secondly, the DS Game Maker user interface (UI) is excellent in terms of ease of use and flexibility. The arrangement of the interface functions and objects are very logical, making things relatively easy to understand.

You can think of DS Game Maker as a visual coding platform. Instead of writing C codes yourself (NDS games are usually written in the C language), DS Game Maker gives you visual menus and forms so you can pick up choices and formulate code logics without writing C codes directly. *DS Game Maker generates the necessary C codes for the actual compilation process.*

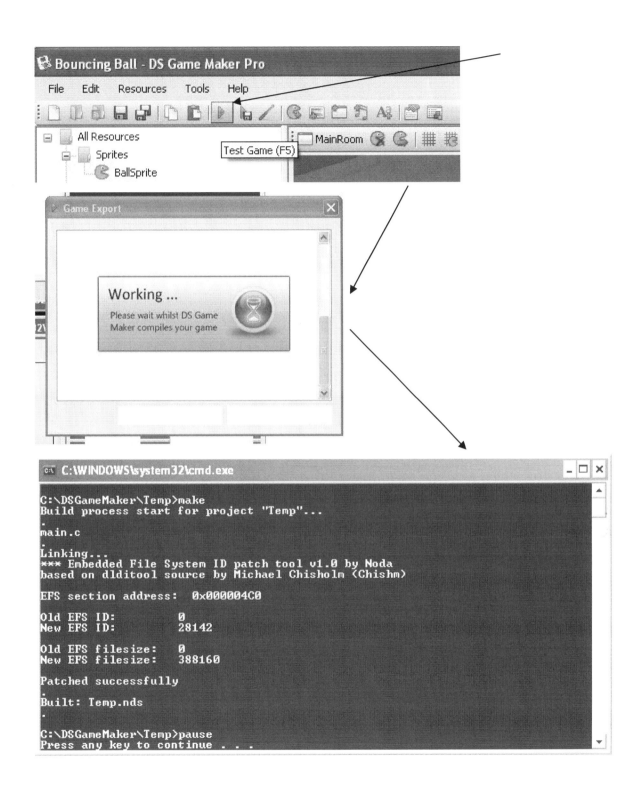

Copyright 2009, 10 **The HobbyPRESS (Hong Kong)**. All rights reserved.

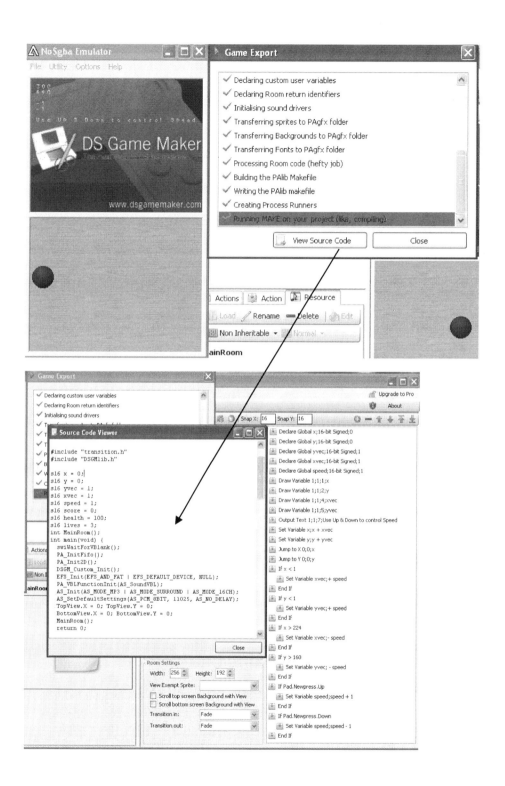

These are the C source codes generated. You do NOT need to understand them in order to use DS Game Maker for game creation.

```
Source Code Viewer                                    _  □  ✕

#include "transition.h"
#include "DSGMlib.h"

s16 x = 0;|
s16 y = 0;
s16 yvec = 1;
s16 xvec = 1;
s16 speed = 1;
s16 score = 0;
s16 health = 100;
s16 lives = 3;
int MainRoom();
int main(void) {
  swiWaitForVBlank();
  PA_InitFifo();
  PA_Init2D();
  DSGM_Custom_Init();
  EFS_Init(EFS_AND_FAT | EFS_DEFAULT_DEVICE, NULL);
  PA_VBLFunctionInit(AS_SoundVBL);
  AS_Init(AS_MODE_MP3 | AS_MODE_SURROUND | AS_MODE_16CH);
  AS_SetDefaultSettings(AS_PCM_8BIT, 11025, AS_NO_DELAY);
  TopView.X = 0; TopView.Y = 0;
  BottomView.X = 0; BottomView.Y = 0;
  MainRoom();
  return 0;

                                              Close
```

Although the C language is efficient and elegant, it is not easy to learn. It was originally developed for gifted programmers, and the learning curve could be real steep. To get a C program to work on NDS, you need to follow exactly the syntax of the language. NOT EASY AT ALL!

Do I need to have R4 in order to use DS Game Maker?

You don't need any special license to use R4. Using R4 is legal as long as you do not use it to run pirated NDS games.

No you don't. DS Game Maker has a third party emulator included so you do not need to use R4 for "actual testing".

R4 is a third party NDS storage device. This kind of device can be used to store work-in-progress images or homebrew video games. You need it because NDS is not shipped with any rewritable storage medium. Older storage devices fit in SLOT-2 and newer devices fit in SLOT-1. R4 goes into SLOT-1.

Slot 2

Slot 1 DS port

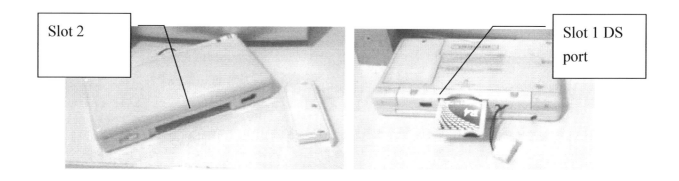

Do I need WiFi support for homebrew game creation?

WiFi provides an alternative means of uploading your homebrew to the NDS without any flashcart. It is NOT a required element of homebrew game creation. In fact, setting up WiFi for this purpose may be a little too complicated for beginners.

Do I need an Emulator box for homebrew game creation?

The Intelligent Systems Emulator box is a special piece of quite expensive hardware for developing NDS games. It is never intended for homebrew and you don't need it for homebrew game creation.

Do I need any special licenses for homebrew game

creation?

No you don't, as long as you are not using any of the official Nintendo development kit (SDK). Illegal use of the copyrighted Nintendo SDK by non-licensed developers is always discouraged.

DS Game Maker is released with several non-official components which have their own license terms. However, none of them really impose any restrictive terms on homebrew game creation.

You may want to review the contents of the 7-zip license and the devkitpro license. Devkitpro is a major component formulating the foundation of the DS Game Maker. It is released under the GPL. The GPL is a copyleft license, meaning that derived works can only be distributed under the same license terms. Simply put, the GPL grants the recipients of the software rights of the free software definition and uses copyleft to ensure the freedoms are preserved, even when the work is changed.

When you are using DS Game Maker to create a game, you are not making commercial deviations out of DS Game Maker. You are simply creating works using DS Game Maker and the libraries of Devkitpro as a foundation. Therefore, it is okay for you to create homebrew games out of it without paying any sort of licensing fees to Devkitpro.

What third party tools are utilized by DS Game Maker?

At the time you install DS Game Maker you will be prompted for installing certain third party tools.

If you review the credits.txt file you will see a list of third party components that run at the backend, primarily for game compilation. You do NOT need to install these components individually by hand.

When creating your homebrew games you are encouraged to give credits accordingly.

Credits.txt
Text Document
4 KB

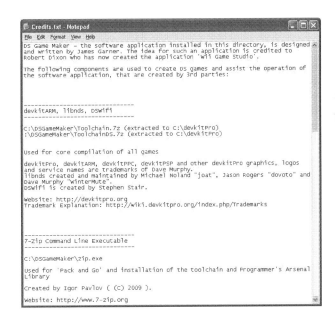

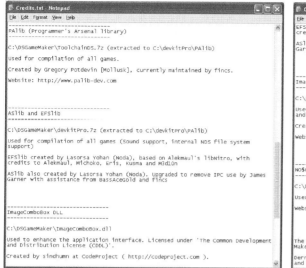

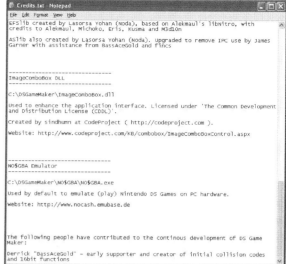

What is "homebrew"? What is DevkitPro?

In the context of NDS game development, homebrew refers to software developed without any official development support. Homebrew projects are usually hobby-oriented. They are not officially endorsed by Nintendo.

This link has a list of homebrew NDS games:
http://www.dev-scene.com/NDS/Games_2007

< NDS

Homebrew Games

Agent Orange

Catch the falling fruits that fall from the tree.. that damned dog!.

Atomix

Build the molecules.

Beyond Good and Evil - Metal Disc

Slide your metal discs to the opponent's side, before he does the same to you.

DevkitPro is the brand name for a collection of toolchains that are commonly used by programmers to create homebrew games.

devkitARM is the component that you may use to build code for NDS. Ds Game Maker uses devkitARM for game compilation. Why ARM? The NDS makes use of two separate ARM processors. There is an ARM9 (ARM946E-S) main CPU as well as an ARM7 (ARM7TDMI) coprocessor, running at clock speeds of 67 MHz and 33 MHz respectively.

NDS has TWO processors running together!

Note that Devkitpro has its own web site. There are active forums over there for you to post questions and comments.

How do I run my NDS game on my PC?

You need to use an emulator. You can download your own emulator, or you can use the emulator that is distributed together with DS Game Maker.

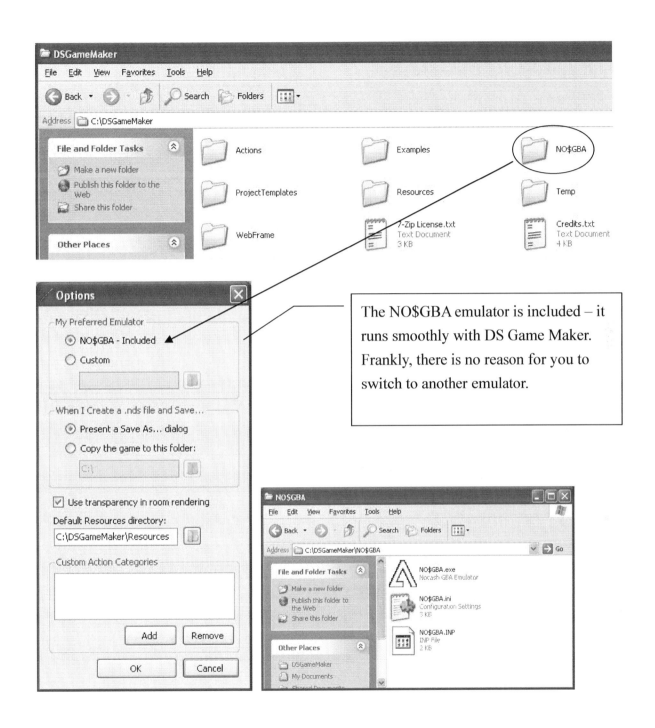

The NO$GBA emulator is included – it runs smoothly with DS Game Maker. Frankly, there is no reason for you to switch to another emulator.

The emulator emulates both screens at the same time.

Homebrew games are typically developed using emulators for convenience (testing can be done without extra hardware). Most emulators are FREE.

Do keep in mind, since the NDS does not come with any storage medium by default, during actual deployment one would need a third-party storage solution to store homebrew.

Can I configure DS Game Maker to use another emulator?

Sure. For example, you can use the DeSmuME emulator.

DeSmuME.exe
NDS(tm) emulator
yopyop

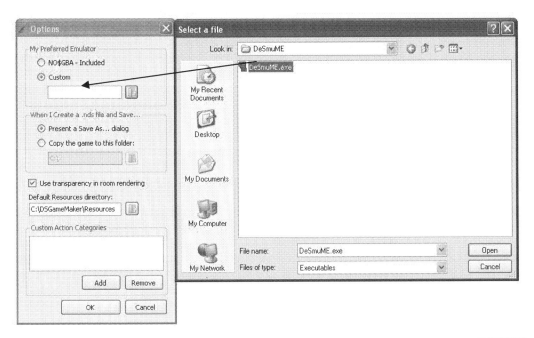

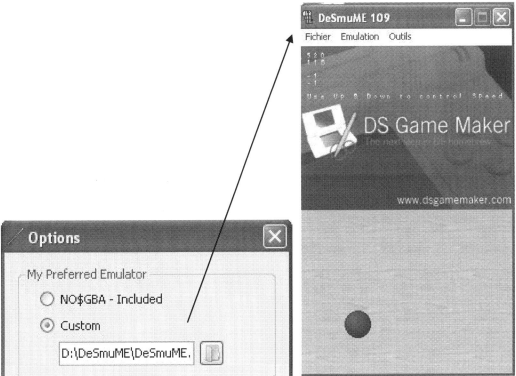

Is DS Game Maker going to be easy if I have rich background in procedural programming languages like C and Pascal?

YES. Even though DS Game Maker will get all C codes generated for you, you would still need to define the game program in pseudo form. You may think of pseudo code as an informal yet high level description of a programming algorithm that has the structural conventions of a programming language – it is way more human readable.

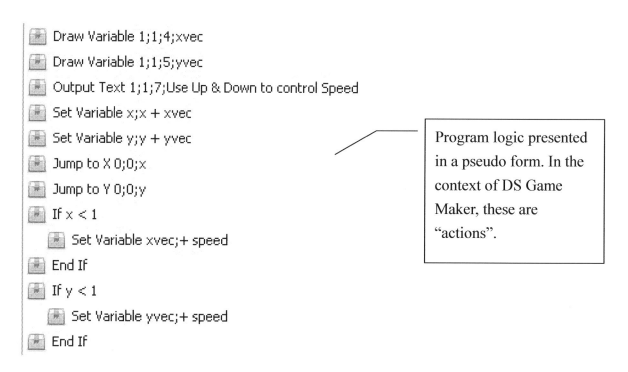

```
Draw Variable 1;1;4;xvec
Draw Variable 1;1;5;yvec
Output Text 1;1;7;Use Up & Down to control Speed
Set Variable x;x + xvec
Set Variable y;y + yvec
Jump to X 0;0;x
Jump to Y 0;0;y
If x < 1
    Set Variable xvec;+ speed
End If
If y < 1
    Set Variable yvec;+ speed
End If
```

> Program logic presented in a pseudo form. In the context of DS Game Maker, these are "actions".

Is DS Game Maker event driven?

Procedural thinking is usually top-down, with heavy focus on procedures and functions. An event driven system, on the other hand, consists of objects with different behaviors and properties, all interacting via events (which in turn would trigger actions). In an event driven environment, a program is structured in terms of events, with no preordered flow of control. Things do NOT start and proceed step by step.

According to the "official" manual, DS Game Maker is NOT exactly an event driven system, but is closer to being procedural.

Why would one prefer DS Game Maker over GM8 for game

creation?

GM8 (Game Maker 8) cannot export games to NDS. There is also no third party export utility capable of doing so.

Why would one prefer DS Game Maker over MMF2 for game creation?

MMF2 (Multimedia Fusion 2) cannot export games to NDS. There is also no third party export utility capable of doing so.

Is DS Game Maker going to be easy if I have rich background in another PC based game creation engine?

May be, and may be not. The thing is that the NDS has way more hardware constraints than a regular PC, therefore you will need to get used to creating game elements under substantial size limitations.

The NDS has 4MBs of main memory plus 656 kilobytes of video memory. It can accommodate at the max 128 sprites together at the same time. The dimensions of your sprites should always correspond to powers of 2. The available texture memory is 512 kb per screen. The max size per texture is 1024x1024 pixels.

Your PC runs at Ghz. The NDS clock speed, on the other hand, is way less than 100mhz.

How does DS Game Maker implement sprite limitation?

When you create a sprite as a resource, it is NOT YET given any index for identifying it later on. You simply give it a UNIQUE name. This name cannot be duplicated.

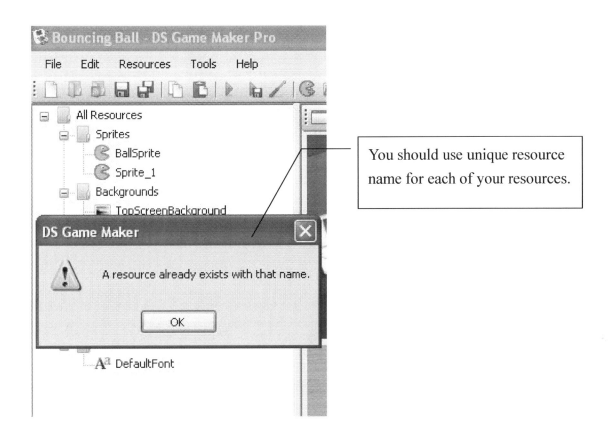

You should use unique resource name for each of your resources.

When you place a sprite into a room, the instance placed in the room will be given a unique index number. The first sprite you place into the room will have an index ID of 0, and so on. The max possible ID value is 127. *An advanced technique: if you have more sprites to display, you should at runtime delete used sprites and free up some IDs for use by the new sprites.*

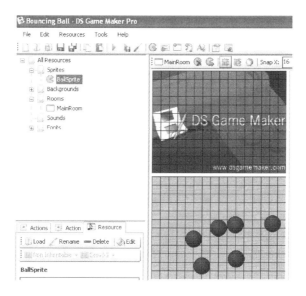

The same sprite can be added into a room multiple times. Each resulting instance of the sprite will be given a unique ID. On the user interface the sprite number is the ID.

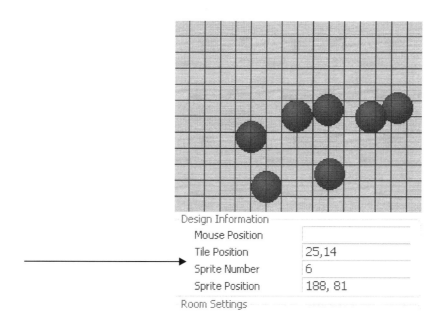

Can I master DS Game Maker without understanding any

programming concept?

Even though DS Game Maker works as a visual tool, its core is no different from a traditional C language development system. The only difference is that you may define the various conditions and actions via a graphical/menu based interface. Still, to effectively plan how the different DS Game Maker resources may interact, you'll need to have a basic sense of program logics. *You do NOT need to know any C language specific program elements and syntaxes though.*

For example, you should know the purpose and use of variables. You should be able to construct IF THEN logics. And you should be able to use simple sprite manipulation functions. You do all these via actions.

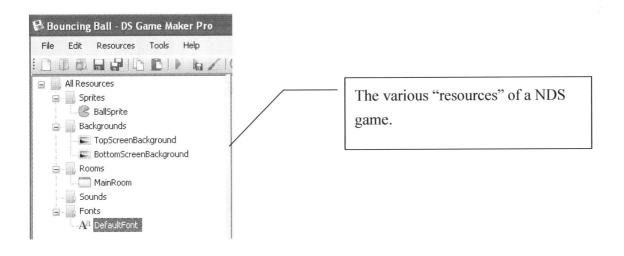

The various "resources" of a NDS game.

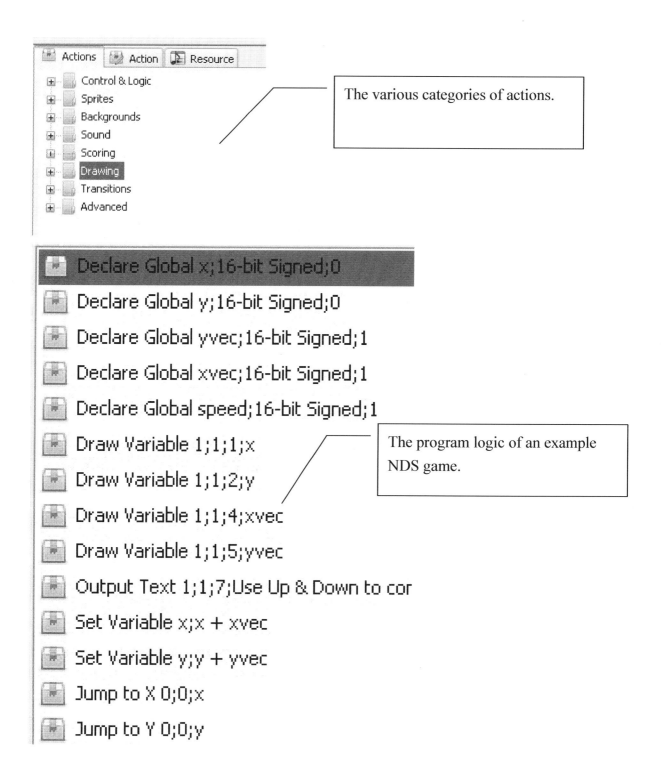

Actions | Action | Resource

- Control & Logic
- Sprites
- Backgrounds
- Sound
- Scoring
- Drawing
- Transitions
- Advanced

The various categories of actions.

Declare Global x;16-bit Signed;0

Declare Global y;16-bit Signed;0

Declare Global yvec;16-bit Signed;1

Declare Global xvec;16-bit Signed;1

Declare Global speed;16-bit Signed;1

Draw Variable 1;1;1;x

Draw Variable 1;1;2;y

Draw Variable 1;1;4;xvec

Draw Variable 1;1;5;yvec

Output Text 1;1;7;Use Up & Down to cor

Set Variable x;x + xvec

Set Variable y;y + yvec

Jump to X 0;0;x

Jump to Y 0;0;y

The program logic of an example NDS game.

Can I write codes in DS Game Maker?

Yes. There is an option which allows you to write custom C codes to create custom program actions.

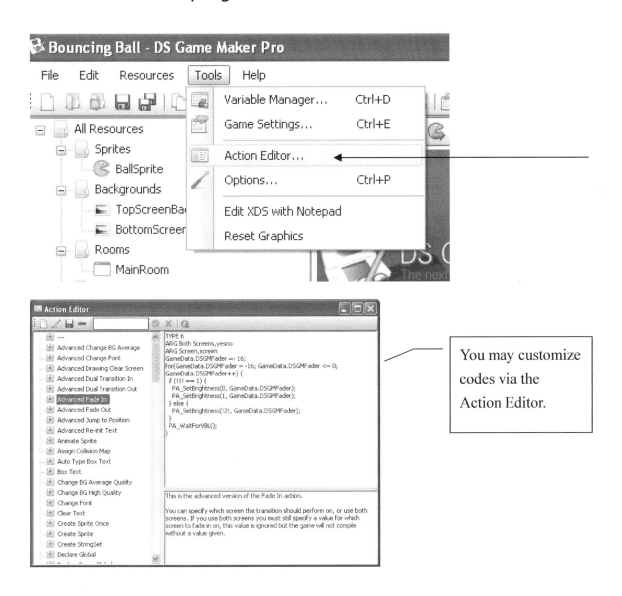

You may customize codes via the Action Editor.

```
TYPE 6
ARG Both Screens,yesno
ARG Screen,screen
GameData.DSGMFader =- 16;
for(GameData.DSGMFader = -16; GameData.DSGMFader <= 0;
GameData.DSGMFader++) {
  if (!1! == 1) {
    PA_SetBrightness(0, GameData.DSGMFader);
    PA_SetBrightness(1, GameData.DSGMFader);
  } else {
    PA_SetBrightness(!2!, GameData.DSGMFader);
  }
  PA_WaitForVBL();
}
```

These are C codes that can be very difficult to read and interpret by beginners.

Separating graphic design from game design...

DS Game Maker does not have its own picture editor. It is going to invoke the default picture editor of your Windows installation at the time you choose to edit a sprite.

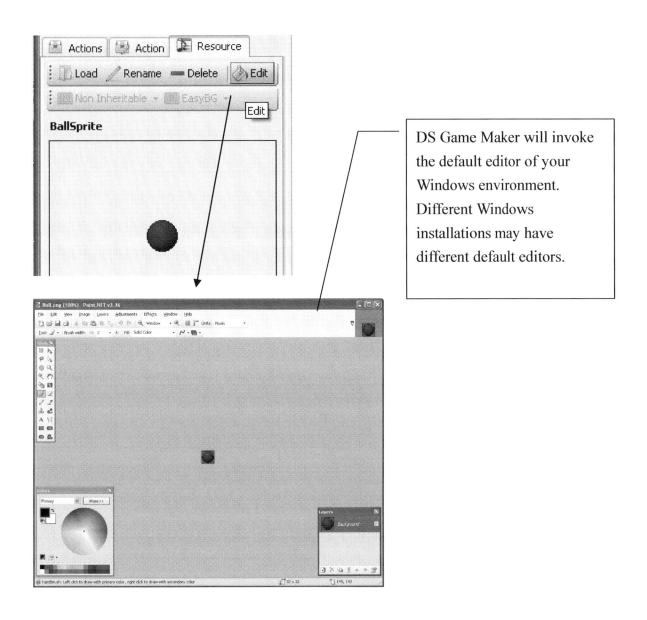

DS Game Maker will invoke the default editor of your Windows environment. Different Windows installations may have different default editors.

Graphic design is a very time consuming process. For an animation to look good you need as many frames as possible. And you need to create animations for different situations in different directions. That means there are MANY frames to create.

Once you are into the graphic and animation work, the entire game creation process will slow down. A common problem is for the programming team to wait for finished artworks and animations from the media team prior to putting things together.

Assuming what you have got is a small team, I would suggest that you clearly break down the game creation process into two sub-processes, with one focusing on the logical "programming" side and another on media (graphics, animation, sound effects...etc) development.

During level design, the programming guy does not really have to use "real stuff". Object actions and events can be designed and implemented through using simple symbolic artworks. For example, instead of waiting for the media design guy to get you a finished Jet you can use a basic plane-like artwork for configuring all the relevant properties, events and actions first.

 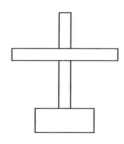

Once the programming works are done and fully tested you may slowly import and "fit in" the real stuff.

For your information, the graphic design guy would need to prepare and implement different animation sequences for the object. The actual use of these sequences is usually determined by the programming guy, through logics implemented in the actions mechanism.

Also for your information, you can always prepare graphics via another paint program, then "export" to DS Game Maker through simple COPY and PASTE.

I am confused – how do the terms Project, Game, Room,

Backgrounds and View relate to each others?

In the context of DS Game Maker game creation:
- a project represents a game
- a project groups all related game resources together
- a room holds a game level
- each game should have at least one room to be playable
- a game shows up through views (camera views)
- each view emulates an NDS screen
- NDS has two screens, therefore you can make use of at the max two views at the same time

- each view can have its own background
- a game can make use of max two views for purpose of game display

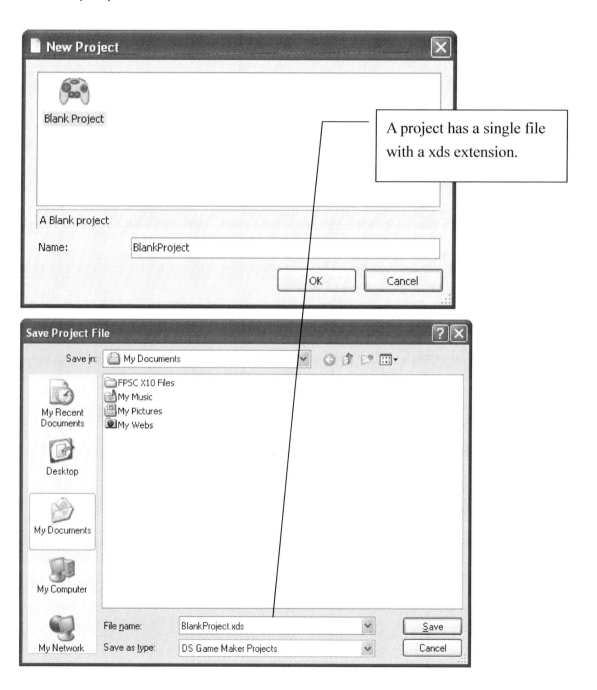

A project has a single file with a xds extension.

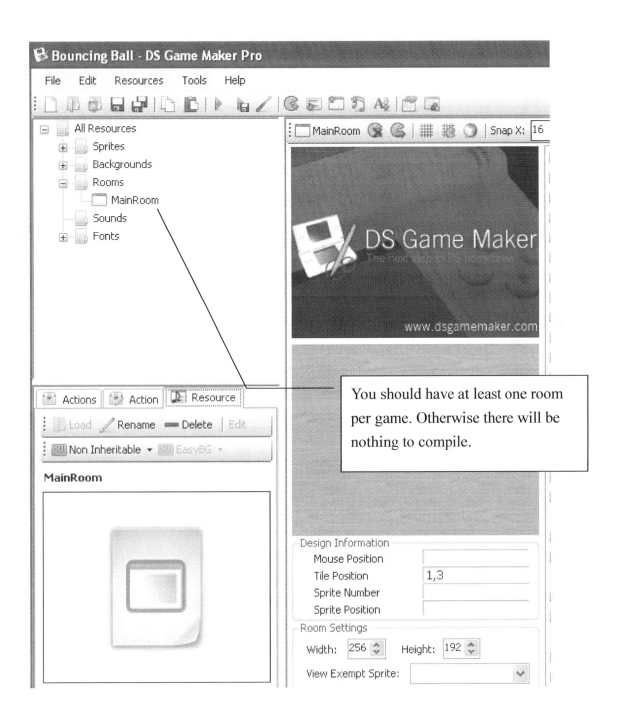

You should have at least one room per game. Otherwise there will be nothing to compile.

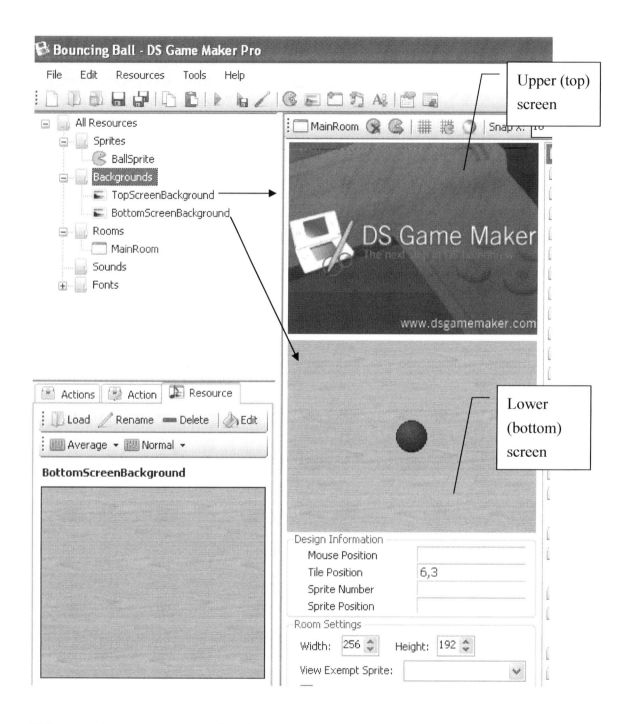

When there are multiple rooms created, you can define the starting room via the Game Settings section:

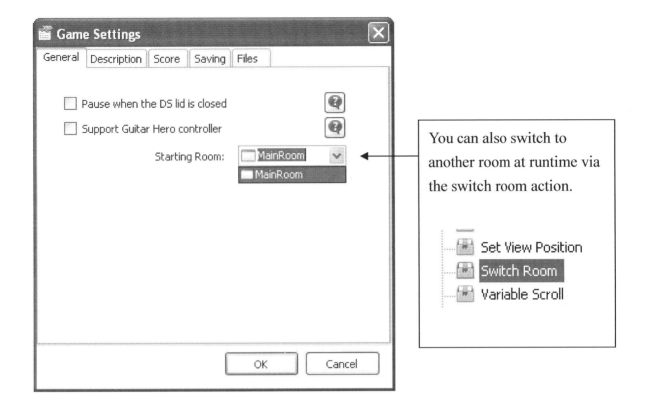

You can also switch to another room at runtime via the switch room action.

How about layers?

On each screen you can have at the max 4 layers for displaying stuff. You have layer 0 – 3 per screen. The lower the layer number the more forward the display would be.

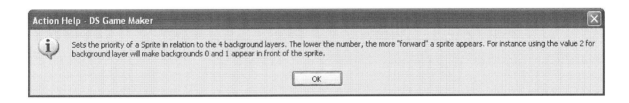

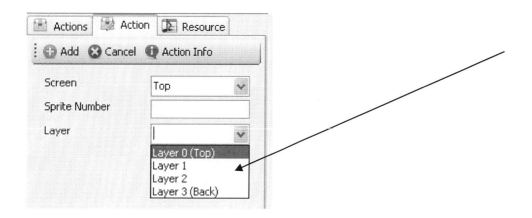

In fact, screen scrolling action can also be performed on a per layer basis.

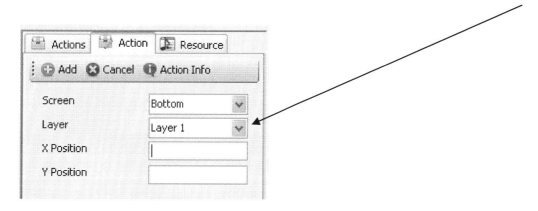

Is screen scrolling possible? Does it have anything to do

with room sizing?

The standard NDS display size is 256 x 192 **per screen**. If your room size is the same as the screen view display size, no scrolling is necessary. However, if your room is larger, scrolling can be enabled as needed, on a per screen basis.

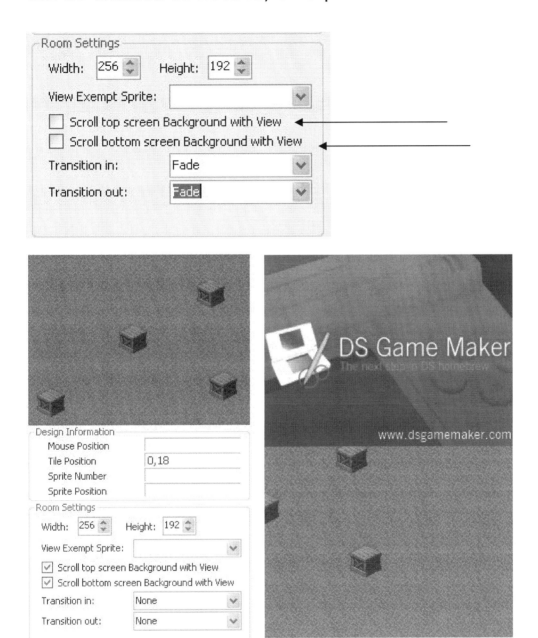

For scrolling to be implemented properly, you should also use a background image which is sufficiently large (at least large enough for scrolling to take place naturally). In fact the author of the software has recommended that the background image should have a width in pixels which is a multiple of 256 pixels.

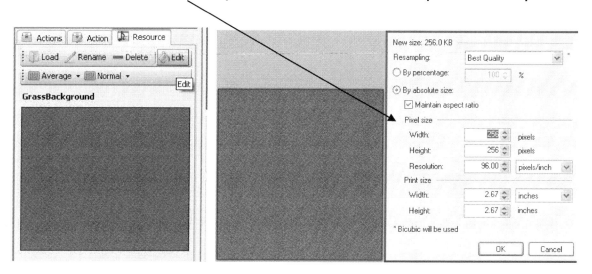

By default, scrolling would not take place across screens. That is, an object would not scroll naturally from the bottom screen to the top screen or vice versa. Scrolling will take place within its own screen only.

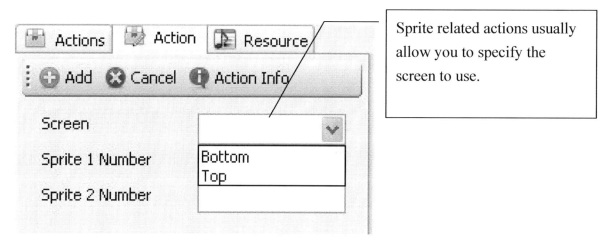

Sprite related actions usually allow you to specify the screen to use.

What are the supported types of resources and the

corresponding file formats?

The supported graphic file types are PNG, GIF and BMP. The example resources that come with DS Game Maker are primarily PNG based. Fonts are also graphic based.

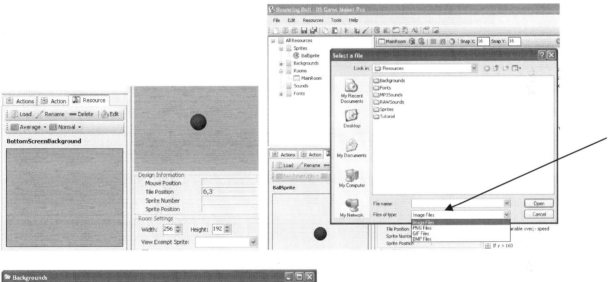

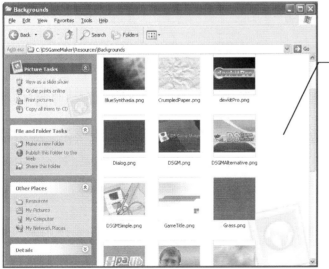

The examples that come with DS Game Maker are mostly in PNG format. For sprite, due to the 256-color limit you may want to opt for the GIF format instead.

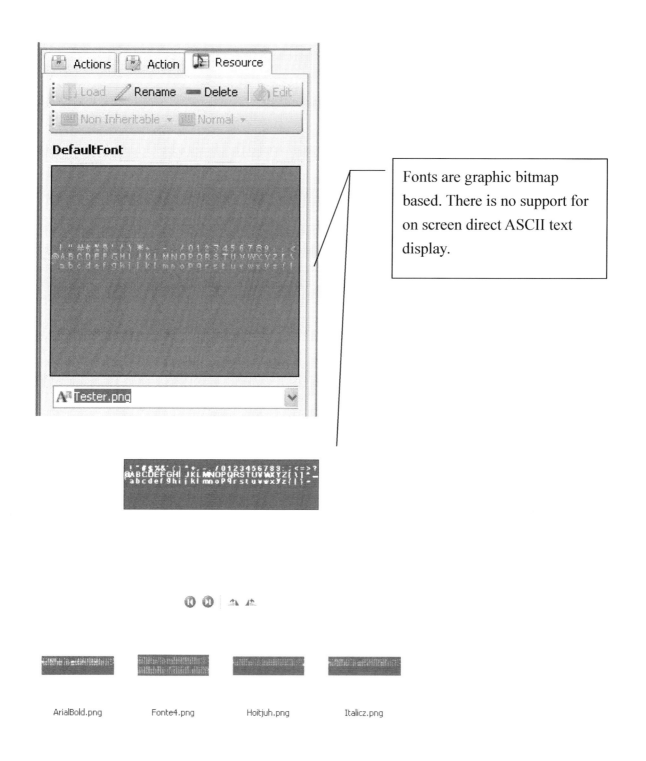

Fonts are graphic bitmap based. There is no support for on screen direct ASCII text display.

ArialBold.png   Fonte4.png   Hoitjuh.png   Italicz.png

Using graphic based fonts doesn't mean you need to paint text in graphic form by hand. You can still use the output text action to specify the textual content.

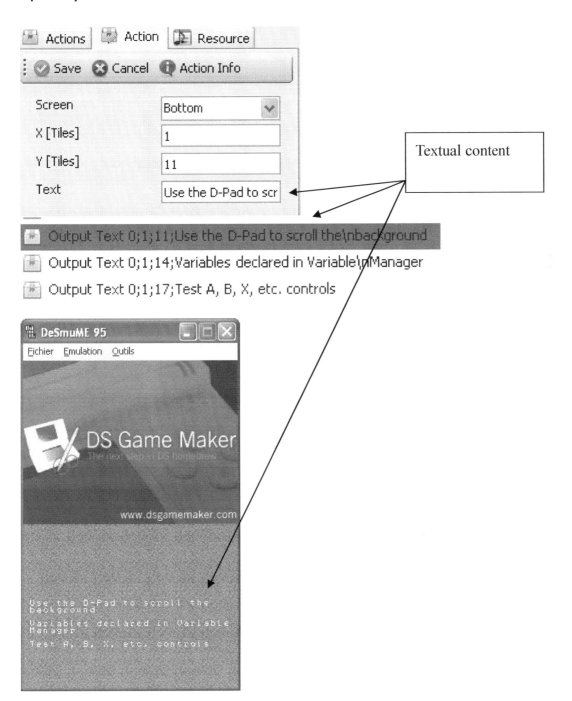

Background musics are MP3 based. Short sound effects are RAW based.

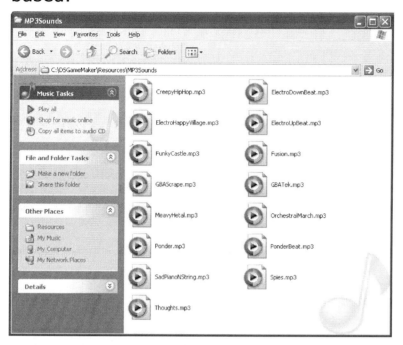

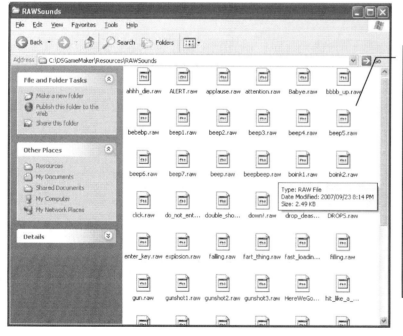

RAW files are quite small in size.

RAW Audio file does not include any header information. Further information on this format is available via http://www.cyanwerks.com/raw-audio-file-formats.html

Sound can be played simply by specifying the sound file to use in your action:

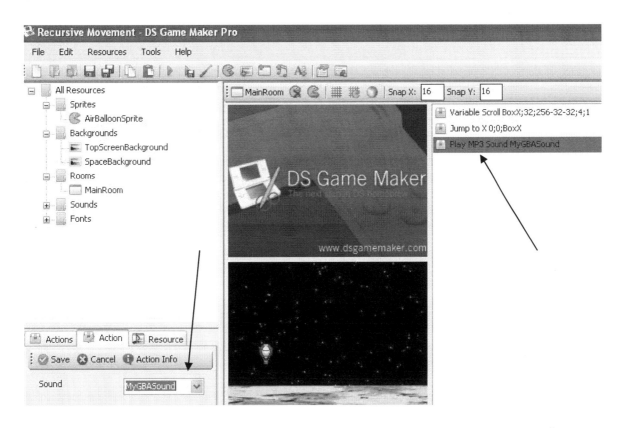

These are the available actions for playing sound files.

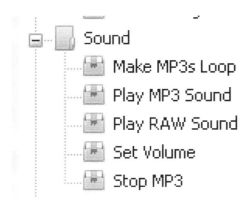

Copyright 2009, 10 **The HobbyPRESS (Hong Kong)**. All rights reserved.

What is special about the NDS format?

Technically speaking, the NDS format is a binary format designed to be run from RAM that is filled from the DS slot 1. It is used by the official game cards as well as most NDS emulators. It has a small header containing a logo, a short description of the actual content, and the two executable binaries needed (one for the ARM7 processor and another for the ARM9 processor).

DS Game Maker can compile your game into the NDS format. However, it does not allow you to open and edit a NDS file. To open and play a NDS file you need to use the emulator.

Development Tools Configuration

What configuration should I use for my DS Game Maker

development station?

A development station for DS Game Maker does not have to be real fast and powerful. DS Game Maker itself is not a power hungry application. The thing is, you may need to do a lot of graphic and animation works. These stuff can eat up processing resources crazily.

I think a reasonable configuration for elementary level game creation in the modern days would entail, at the least, a P4 processor, 2GB RAMs, 100GB+ hard disk ...etc. I always recommend that you have at least TWO hard disks installed on the same computer, with Norton GHOST (a disk cloning program) in place to create a complete image of your primary disk so if something goes wrong you can recover the development settings quickly by restoring from the image.

Working data backup is different – you need to regularly backup your working data into at least TWO different places, such as a high capacity SD card and a USB connected external hard disk. SCSI, IDE, SATA... all these don't really matter. DS Game Maker will not run better just because it is on a SCSI disk.

You will need a card reader. When you compile your game using DS Game Maker, you will end up with a .nds file. With a DS flashcart you can put this file on and run it on an actual NDS.

What is the recommended disk layout for my DS Game

Maker development station?

Personally I would suggest that you maintain the following partitions:
- a partition for the Windows OS
- a partition for DS Game Maker and all other development tools
- a partition for all the working data (game graphics, the game

application files, sound effect files ...etc)

If you have a second hard disk, on this second disk you should have:
- a partition for Norton Ghost to build and keep clone images
- a partition for making backups of the working data
- a partition for Windows virtual memory (i.e. disk swapping)
- a partition for special purpose swapping (when you need to use some heavy duty graphic processing applications)

How much disk space should I keep for DS Game Maker?

Full installation takes approximately 26MB.

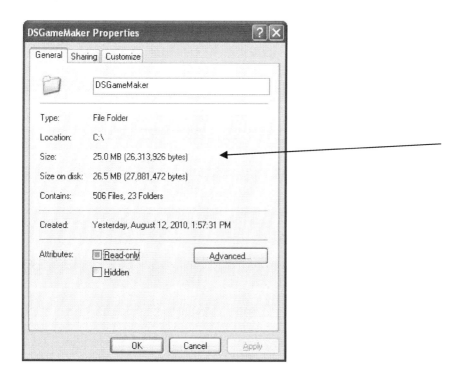

By default, the DS Game Maker program has the following folder structure:

Because you may want to install additional tools or resources at a later time, I would say you better keep several hundred MBs of free space for everything related to your game project.

How do I verify my installation?

One easiest way to ensure proper installation of everything DS Game Maker related is to test compile an example game. There are a bunch of example projects that come with DS Game Maker. Pick one, then build a NDS file out of it to see if things can proceed smoothly.

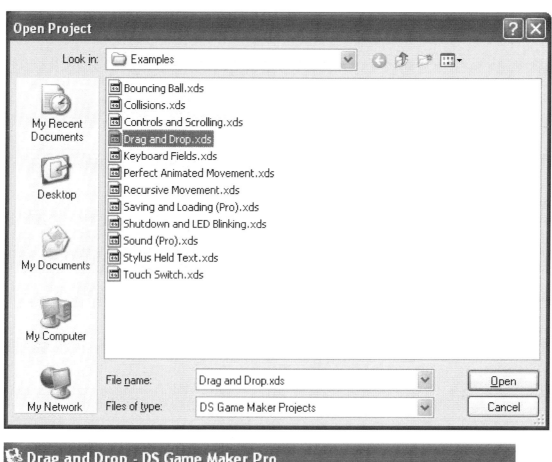

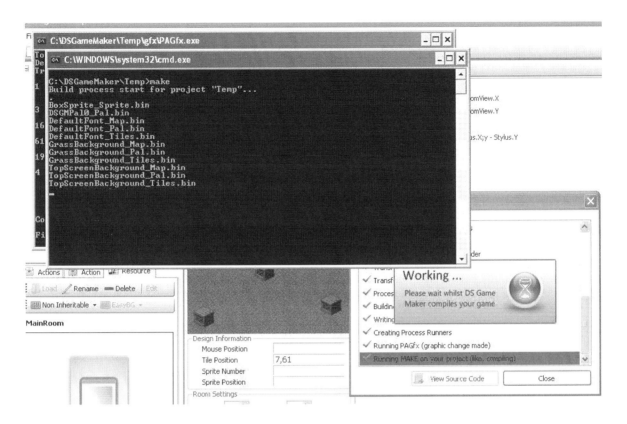

If there are problems with your installation, compilation will fail, and you may need to reinstall the software (or the toolchain at the least). Otherwise, a NDS file will be built successfully.

You may choose to reinstall just the toolchain and see if the errors can be fixed.

You do need to realize that compilation failure may be due to your errors (in this case there is no need to re-install anything). For example, when you use an action without supplying the necessary arguments, compilation can fail (you will be warned beforehand). If your code has error (a design problem), you will receive an error prompt too.

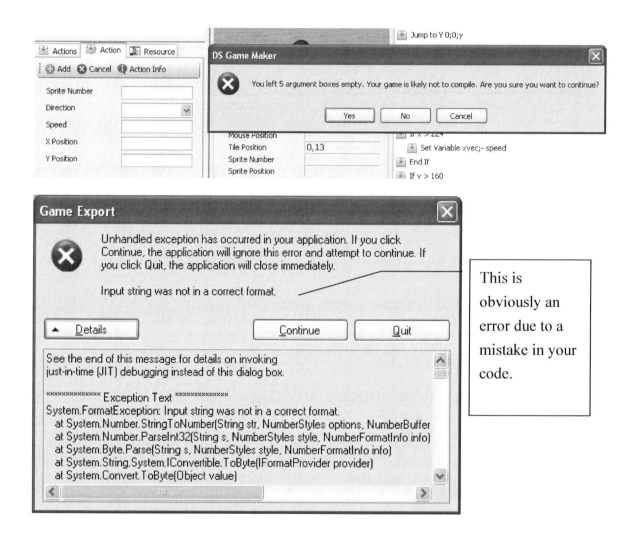

This is obviously an error due to a mistake in your code.

DS Game Maker does not always catch error at design time. However, serious syntax problem due to improper action arrangement will fail the compilation process early:

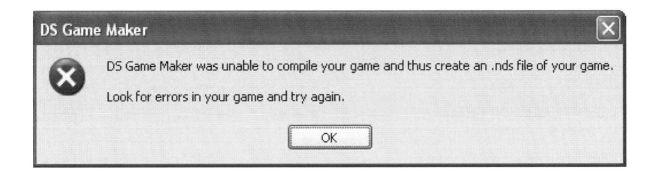

Do I have to use FAT as the file system for running DS

Game Maker?

No you don't. NDS itself uses FAT as the file system for storage. That means if you are transferring your homebrew to the actual NDS via a flashcart then the flashcart will have to be formatted as FAT.

DS Game Maker runs on Windows and the design time filesystem simply does not matter. If you are running Windows XP or beyond, you will most likely use NTFS anyway.

Design time performance VS runtime performance

Design-end performance VS user-end performance

When you plan your development station configuration, keep in mind that design time performance boost is not the same as runtime performance improvement.

Design time performance boost improves productivity (your tools run faster), while runtime performance boost allows the game you create to run faster on the client end.

If your game is going to have a large number of super fancy graphics and animations plus tons of rich objects all showing up at the same time, NDS will for sure have a harder time working things out. The key issue is this – when you have a very fast development station, all games can run fast in front of you. This can actually mislead you into believing that your game could run as smooth on the NDS.

Just keep this in mind, the NDS is way less powerful than your PC! Clock-speed wise, NDS is MUCH MUCH slower.

What amount of memory should I install in my DS Game

Maker development station? Do I need a dual core

processor?

Along the process of game creation, you often need to keep multiple applications (graphics, effects, game…etc) running at the same time, therefore the more RAM you have the better (and RAM is dirt cheap these days anyway).

DS Game Maker is a 32bit based platform. It runs on 32bit based Windows. The maximum amount of memory that can be utilized by a 32bit Windows is roughly 3.3GB. Therefore, practically speaking a 3GB configuration would be all that you need. Most modern motherboards can let you install 3GBs or more of RAM (2GB + 1GB or 1GB + 1GB + 1GB).

DS Game Maker itself was NOT written to take advantage of multiple processor cores. Therefore, if you are running only DS Game Maker and nothing else then there would be no performance gain by using dual core processor. HOWEVER, as said before along the process of game creation you will very likely need to keep multiple applications running at the same time. Therefore, you may find a dual core processor beneficial.

In fact you can monitor CPU utilization via the Windows Task Manager. You can press CTRL ALT DEL to activate it.

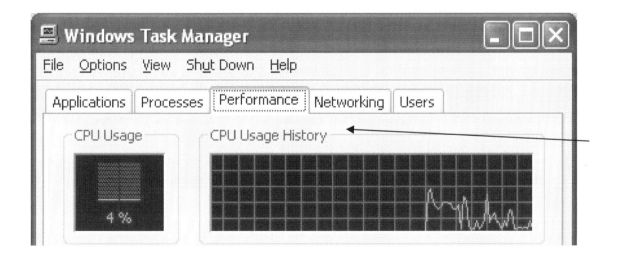

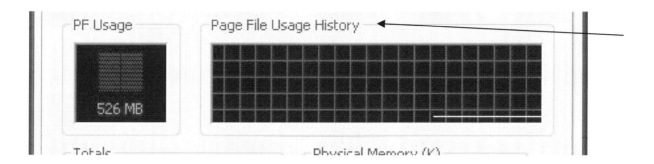

Do this when DS Game Maker is running. If you see constantly high utilization here (80% or higher), a processor upgrade may become necessary. If you see heavy page file usage from the line chart, that means disk swapping is frequent – you don't have sufficient RAM in the system.

DS Game Maker is NOT processor/memory intensive so the chance of over-utilization is minimal. In fact, high utilization may be due to reasons totally outside of the running of DS Game Maker.

If for whatever reason the DS Game Maker is running at a very high utilization rate, restart the system and the rate should drop immediately.

How do I optimize DS Game Maker on my development station?

First of all you need to identify the processes that belong to DS Game Maker. You can do this via the Windows Task Manager.

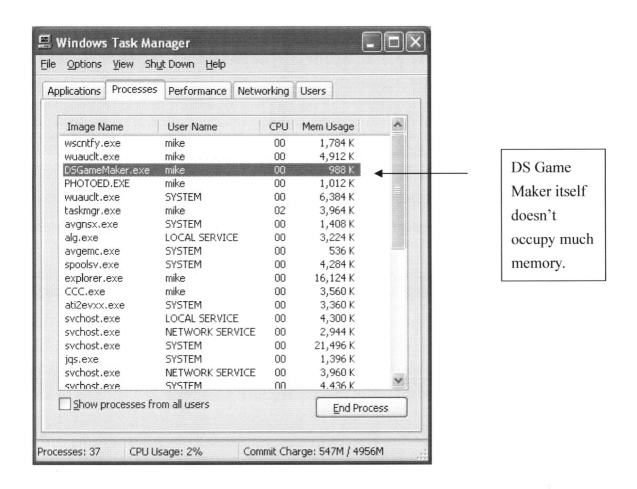

DS Game Maker itself doesn't occupy much memory.

You can right click on the relevant processes and set the proper priority. By default the priority level is Normal. You may try to set it to High. *A "High" value here should not lead to system instability. A "Realtime" value, however, should be discouraged.*

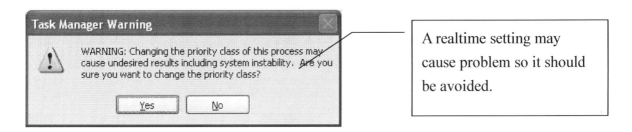

A realtime setting may cause problem so it should be avoided.

Do I need a high performance graphic card in my DS Game

Maker development station?

Generally speaking, onboard integrated graphic display is slower than a dedicated display card. This holds true for ALL windows applications.

DS Game Maker is not demanding in terms of graphic display power. And there are no fancy 3D effects involved. Therefore, any modern graphic display unit will do. I personally prefer dedicated display cards simply because they have their very own onboard RAM so the main system memory can be conserved (no need to share memory with the display function).

Do I need a large chunk of Video RAM on my graphic card

to support DS Game Maker?

DS Game Maker does not specifically ask for a particular amount of Video RAM. You cannot deploy true or high color on NDS anyway. The NDS color palette is relatively limited (32256 color at the max). For sprite, you can have max 256-color on each, which is even more restrictive.

Do I need DirectX 9 or DirectX 10 installed?

No you don't. NDS games never require DirectX support.

Which Windows version should be used to power my DS

Game Maker development station?

My personal recommendation is Windows XP. It is stable and reasonably reliable. Vista itself is way too power hungry. It eats up half of all system resources even when not running anything. Windows Server 2003 is never optimized for front end applications. Windows 7 is too new and I have not been able to test it out.

System:

   Microsoft Windows XP
   Professional
   Version 2002
   Service Pack 2

Registered to:

You should use a 32-bit Windows. If you use a 64-bit Windows to run DS Game Maker, it may actually be slower since the OS must perform a bunch of compatibility processing works at the background.

What other development tools should I install on my computer?

DS Game Maker has no built-in picture editor. The Windows's default graphic editor (Paint) is a pretty basic one. To create very fancy graphics you'll need something more powerful. The Paint.NET software by dotPDN LLC is free and is very powerful so I would not hesitate to recommend it.

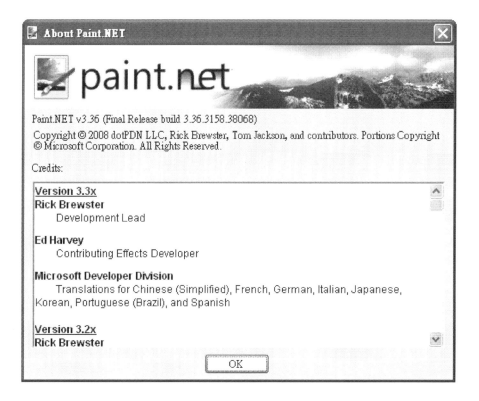

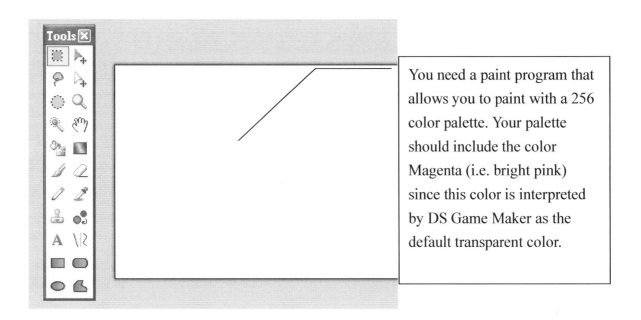

You need a paint program that allows you to paint with a 256 color palette. Your palette should include the color Magenta (i.e. bright pink) since this color is interpreted by DS Game Maker as the default transparent color.

You also need a good virus scanner for proper virus protection. AVG is free is and is pretty reliable.

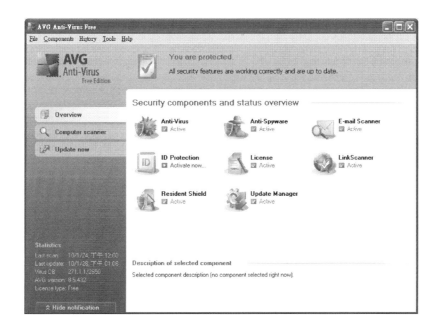

What tool can I use to open texture files of another format and convert them for further manipulation?

You need a conversion tool. One such tool is the LS Image Converter from Linos Software:

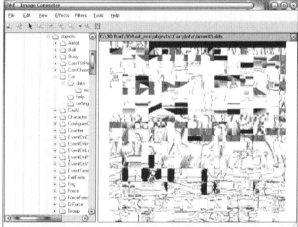

The Image Converter currently supports these image types:
IMPORT - PDF, PSD, PS, EPS, WBMP, WMF, EMF, PIC, JP2, JLS, FPX, RAW, DCM, CUT, IFF, DDS, PBM, PGM, PPM, RAF, RAS, XMB, XPB
EXPORT - BMP, JPEG, GIF, TIF, PNG, PCX, ICO, TGA, PSD, PS, EMF, JP2, FPX, RAW, PBM, PGM, PPM, XPB.

Smoothdraw is a paint program that can read files in a wide range of formats for further editing.

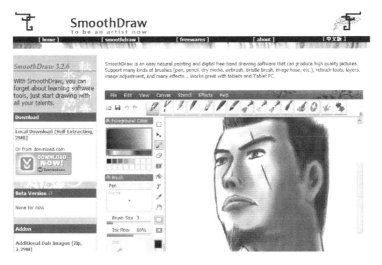

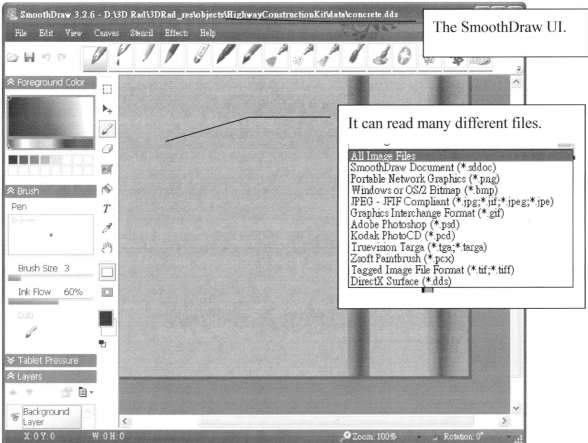

The SmoothDraw UI.

It can read many different files.

All Image Files
SmoothDraw Document (*.sddoc)
Portable Network Graphics (*.png)
Windows or OS/2 Bitmap (*.bmp)
JPEG - JFIF Compliant (*.jpg;*.jif;*.jpeg;*.jpe)
Graphics Interchange Format (*.gif)
Adobe Photoshop (*.psd)
Kodak PhotoCD (*.pcd)
Truevision Targa (*.tga;*.targa)
Zsoft Paintbrush (*.pcx)
Tagged Image File Format (*.tif;*.tiff)
DirectX Surface (*.dds)

If my hard drive crashes, what special procedures are necessary so I can reinstall DS Game Maker?

You may reinstall DS Game Maker from the downloaded file at any time. No special procedure of any sort is necessary. To upgrade to the PRO edition, however, you must activate again using your email address and serial code.

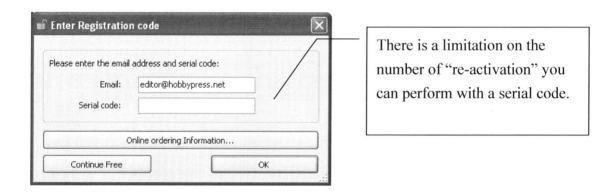

There is a limitation on the number of "re-activation" you can perform with a serial code.

Can I run DS Game Maker without network connection?

In theory you can. HOWEVER, an active internet connection can let you search for help as needed so there is no reason to go without it.

Are the DS Game Maker application files vulnerable to

virus attack?

As of the time of this writing, to the best of my knowledge there is no specific virus attack targeting the DS Game Maker application files (in XDS format). Still, for your peace of mind it is best to have a proper anti-virus solution in place.

Performance Concerns

What is the optimal display resolution and color depth for

DS Game Maker to operate at design time?

Any resolution you feel comfort to work with. The higher the resolution the more workload your display card would have to handle. Most modern display cards, however, will do just fine at 1024 x 768 OR 1280 x 1024. In terms of color depth, you may simply stay with what you already have in your Windows OS.

What is the optimal color depth for DS Game Maker

created game to operate at runtime?

Talking about color-depth, the general theory is that when you have more color to display then slower overall display performance will result.

256-color is the max limit for sprite (yes, the color palette is pretty restrictive). Keep in mind, a good game doesn't always have to be very "colorful". Also, different sprites can use different palettes, making it possible to work around the limitations in a way.

Game Design

What is the proper way of using variables?

A variable can be thought of as a value that has a name attached to it. The value of a variable can be changed at runtime, and the current value of the variable at any point can be easily referred to by simply stating the variable name.

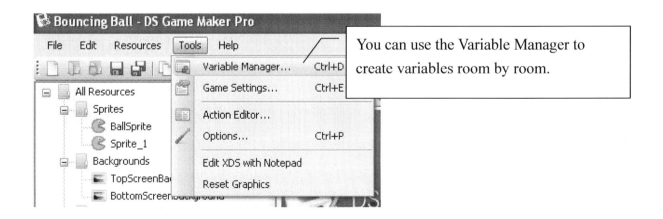

You can use the Variable Manager to create variables room by room.

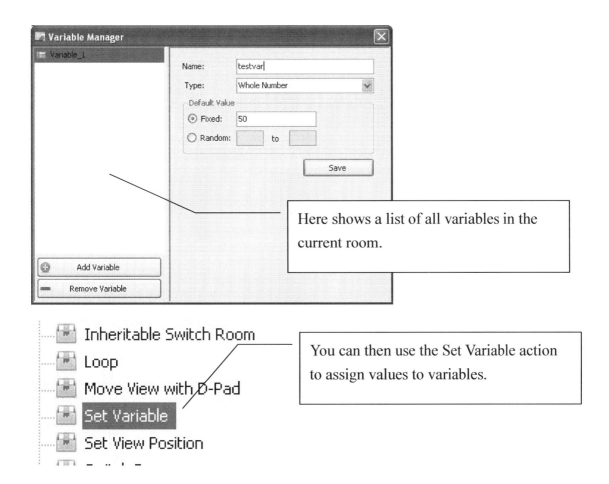

Here shows a list of all variables in the current room.

You can then use the Set Variable action to assign values to variables.

You want to know that a variable is NOT a DS Game Maker resource.

It is a good practice to give a variable a unique and meaningful name. You want to make it easy to deduce the purpose of a variable given a variable name only. Avoid accented characters or other weird symbolic characters in variable names since they are never descriptive.

You should pick a consistent naming convention and stick to it. If you cannot think of a good descriptive set of names for your variables, do not just make up some random names. Unpronounceable names should particularly be avoided.

You should begin variables with a lowercase letter. Using mixed case (both uppercase and lowercase) is fine as long as this is a style that is being used consistently throughout the game codes. Variable names should contain only letters, numbers, and underscores. Generally speaking, it is never a good idea to begin variable names with numbers or underscores.

Single-character variable names should be avoided whenever possible.

It can be VERY confusing to have too many variable types in use. Keep in mind, using the right variable type is as important as making your code correct and accurate.

There are many types of value that can be assigned to a variable. HOWEVER, you do not want to make things unnecessarily complicated.

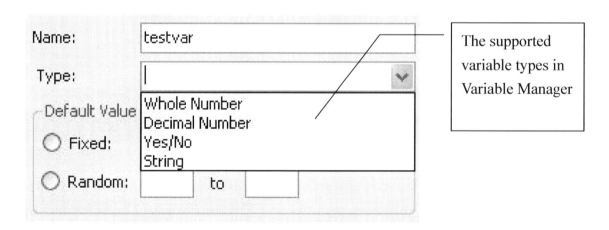

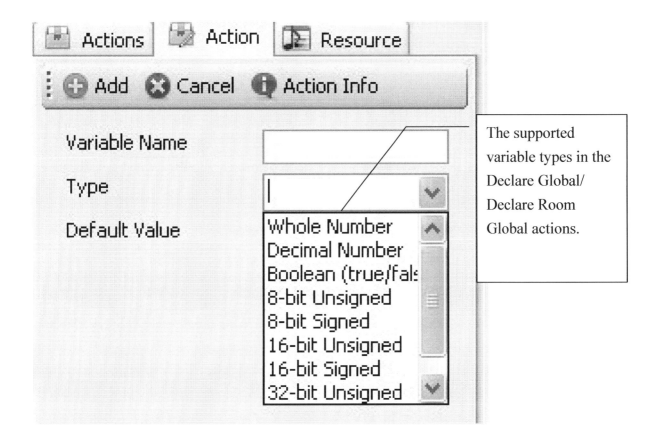

The supported variable types in the Declare Global/ Declare Room Global actions.

For the purpose of game creation, you should not need to use anything other than integer whole number and text string (or a single textual character). Technically DS Game Maker supports real number (decimal allowed) but I think for game use integer (whole number) is mostly sufficient.

Variables for use in a room can be defined via the Variable Manager. Once you have a variable defined in there, you can use the set variable action to assign value to it.

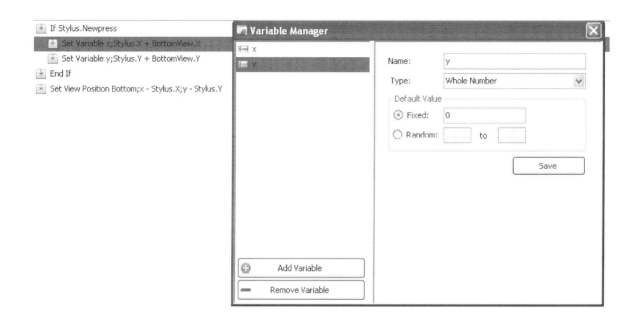

An integer is a simple whole number. You can use it to keep track of location information, health information, score, item inventory ...etc. You can also use integer values to represent logical elements, such as 0=true, 1=false, 2=neutral, 3 = unknown ...etc.   A text string, on the other hand, can be used to communicate textual message.

Integers are whole numbers without any decimal points. They can be negative or positive. Real numbers are floating-point numbers - that is, numbers with decimal points and fraction digits.

You do not need to use anything to embrace an integer value. You do need to use quotes to embrace a text string value.

If a variable is expected to be global (one that is accessible everywhere throughout the entire game, across rooms), make it global.

In DS Game Maker, there is no "local variable". A relatively "local" scope is known as a room global. A room global variable is one that can be accessed throughout the entire room. **It is a variable local to a particular room.**

To create a global variable, you need to declare it as such. On the other hand, if you want to use variables only within the current room (quite often these variables are for temporary calculation use only), you should NOT make them global. Global variables always stay alive to consume memory.

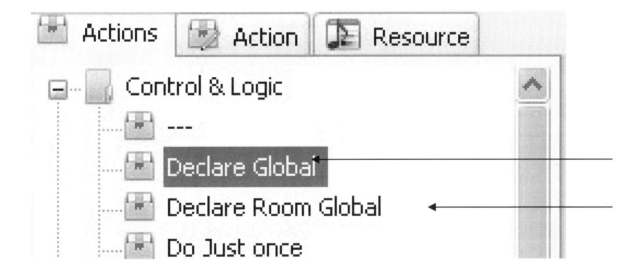

If you use the Declare actions to define global variables, you do not need to use the Variable Manager to define them again.

Declare Global x;16-bit Signed;0

Declare Global y;16-bit Signed;0

Declare Global yvec;16-bit Signed;1

Declare Global xvec;16-bit Signed;1

Declare Global speed;16-bit Signed;1

What is going to happen if I do NOT declare a variable?

```
C:\WINDOWS\system32\cmd.exe                                    _ □ ×

C:\DSGameMaker\Temp>make
Build process start for project "Temp"...

DefaultFont_Map.bin
DefaultFont_Pal.bin
DefaultFont_Tiles.bin
main.c
c:/DSGameMaker/Temp/source/main.c: In function 'Room_1':
c:/DSGameMaker/Temp/source/main.c:56: error: 'displayCount' undeclared (first us
e in this function)
c:/DSGameMaker/Temp/source/main.c:56: error: (Each undeclared identifier is repo
rted only once
c:/DSGameMaker/Temp/source/main.c:56: error: for each function it appears in.)
make[1]: *** [main.o] Error 1
make: *** [build] Error 2

C:\DSGameMaker\Temp>pause
Press any key to continue . . .
```

You will receive an error during compilation. All variables need to be declared.

How to assign values to my variables?

You can use the set variable action.

Set Variable testvar;123

The help message below tells exactly how different types of variables should have their values properly assigned.

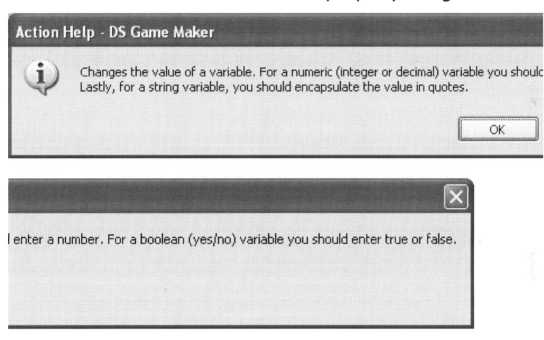

Action Help - DS Game Maker

Changes the value of a variable. For a numeric (integer or decimal) variable you should Lastly, for a string variable, you should encapsulate the value in quotes.

OK

I enter a number. For a boolean (yes/no) variable you should enter true or false.

For numeric variables, it is always possible to change values using these mathematical operators: *, +, - and / .

How to show values of my variables?

The easiest way is to use the draw variable action. You need to specify the position of the drawing and the variable to draw. You must define the drawing variable by variable.

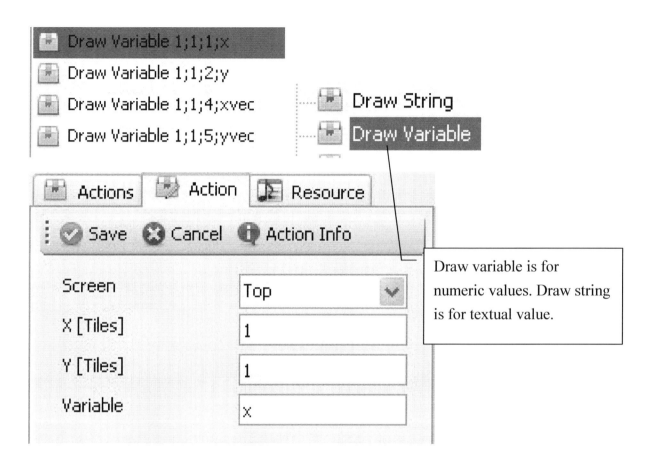

Draw variable is for numeric values. Draw string is for textual value.

What is initialization all about?

To initialize a variable means to give it a default value. While not mandatory, you want to do this explicitly to avoid any future guess works. Variable Manager can let you do this at the time of variable creation:

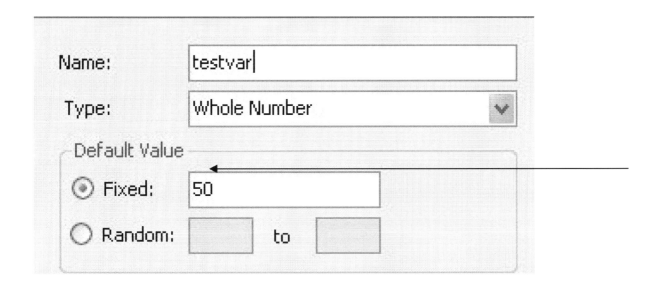

You may also use the DECLARE action, especially when the variable is to be setup as a global one.

What are control statements?

Control Statements provide ways for you to control what parts of the game are to be executed at certain times. The syntaxes of DS Game Maker actions are quite similar to regular English. They can be classified as branching statements and loops. You may not always use loop in your game. However, you will very like use quite many IF conditions.

Knowledge on computer programming will be helpful here.

How are IF conditions constructed? What are the pitfalls?

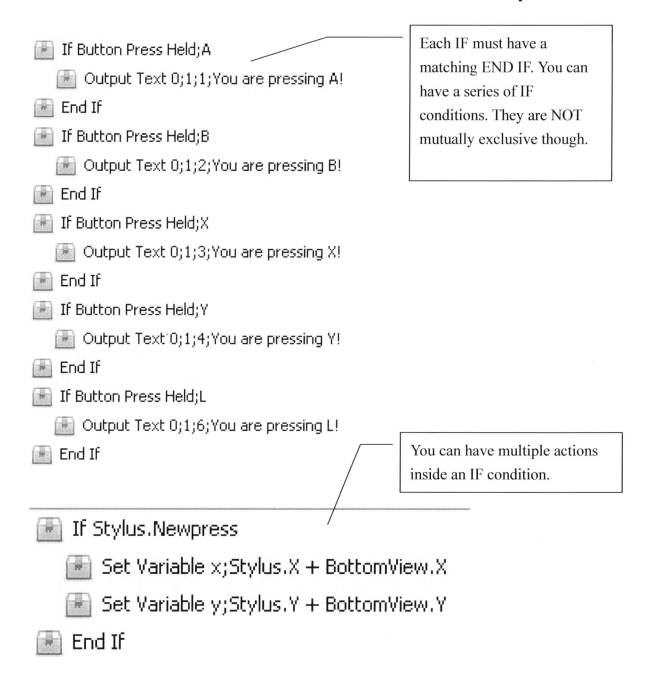

If Button Press Held;A
    Output Text 0;1;1;You are pressing A!
End If
If Button Press Held;B
    Output Text 0;1;2;You are pressing B!
End If
If Button Press Held;X
    Output Text 0;1;3;You are pressing X!
End If
If Button Press Held;Y
    Output Text 0;1;4;You are pressing Y!
End If
If Button Press Held;L
    Output Text 0;1;6;You are pressing L!
End If

> Each IF must have a matching END IF. You can have a series of IF conditions. They are NOT mutually exclusive though.

> You can have multiple actions inside an IF condition.

If Stylus.Newpress
    Set Variable x;Stylus.X + BottomView.X
    Set Variable y;Stylus.Y + BottomView.Y
End If

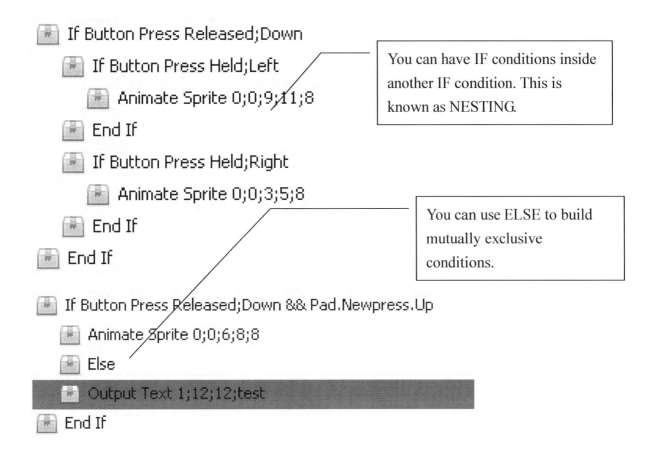

If Button Press Released;Down
   If Button Press Held;Left
      Animate Sprite 0;0;9;11;8
   End If
   If Button Press Held;Right
      Animate Sprite 0;0;3;5;8
   End If
End If

If Button Press Released;Down && Pad.Newpress.Up
   Animate Sprite 0;0;6;8;8
   Else
      Output Text 1;12;12;test
End If

> You can have IF conditions inside another IF condition. This is known as NESTING.

> You can use ELSE to build mutually exclusive conditions.

When using IF, you will encounter error when there is missing ENDIF. Also, it is very easy to have logical mistakes. Logical mistakes may not lead to compilation failure. They will, however, very likely lead to bug. For example, some IF conditions may never come true if you place them in the wrong place. Remember, the actions are being processed from top to down sequentially. Also, with the use of ELSE the conditions become mutually exclusive so an improper condition may lead to the same result every time the action is executed. You may also receive error when the improper comparison operator is used.

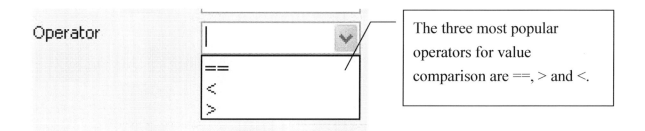

Operator — The three most popular operators for value comparison are ==, > and <.

The value of variables can be compared (conditional testing) through IF statements. **IF statements can be used to allow the flow of the game to be changed (branching).** Without such a conditional statement, a game would run almost the exact same way every time. An IF statement can test for a condition and then execute code based on whether that condition is true or untrue. If the condition is true, the code flow will branch one way. If the condition is untrue, no branching will take place

When you place one control statement inside of another control statement, nesting is said to have taken place. You can have IF inside IF, but make sure you don't mess up the logic flow – it is very easy to confuse yourself when there are too many levels of nesting in your codes.

An IF action requires that you manually type in the condition yourself. You can use && to specify an AND condition (that means there are two elements to be satisfied to fulfill the condition).

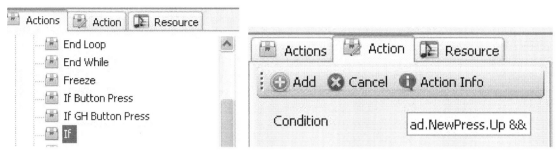

AND is going to return TRUE if all conditions are TRUE. This AND operator is sometimes written as &&. OR is different. If either or both of the two conditions are TRUE then it will return TRUE. This OR operator is sometimes written as || (pipe characters). Do note that having multiple ANDs in an IF statement is NOT the same as using multiple IF statements. The purpose is simply different.

It is very easy to build a problematic condition this way:

Can both of these really happen together?

The IF BUTTON PRESSED action is way easier and less confusing to use for detecting user input and building proper corresponding action.

You can also construct an IF condition based on the location of a sprite. However, the X and Y positions will need to be tested separately:

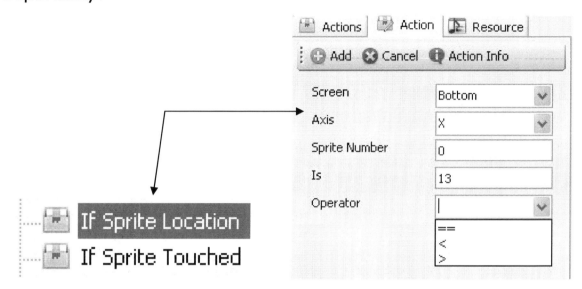

Any guidelines in making comments?

The comments should be capable of clarifying your code actions. They should be written to give clean and clear overviews of codes and provide additional information that is not present in there. They should only contain information that is relevant to reading and understanding your game. You should state clearly the purpose and use of your code actions right at the beginning. Revisions of code action should be marked in there too. Commenting of non-obvious design decisions is always encouraged.

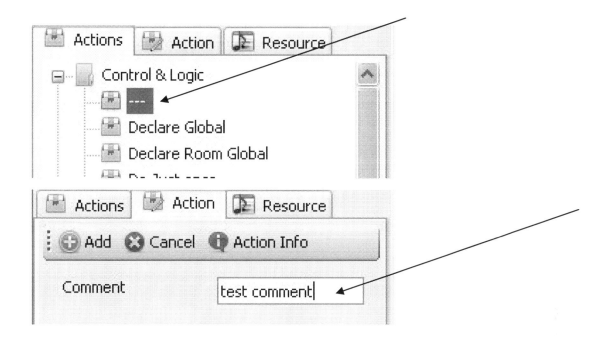

You can insert comments anywhere within the room codes.

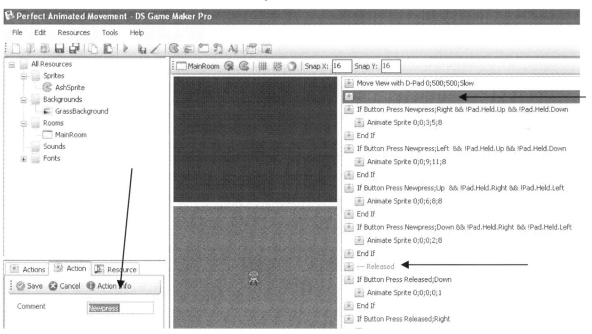

What is a D-Pad? What about a stylus? How do I use them

to control sprite and view movement?

The D Pad is the + shape control. The stylus refers to the pen.

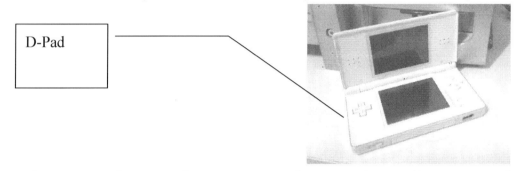

The Move Sprite with D-Pad action can be used to allow D-Pad control over a sprite's movement:

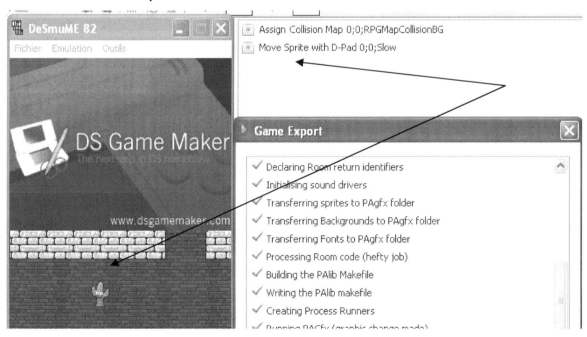

You need to know that moving a sprite is different from setting a position of a sprite. If you set a position, it jumps directly to the specified position without going through the movement action.

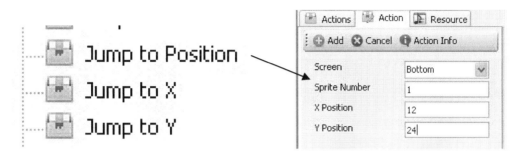

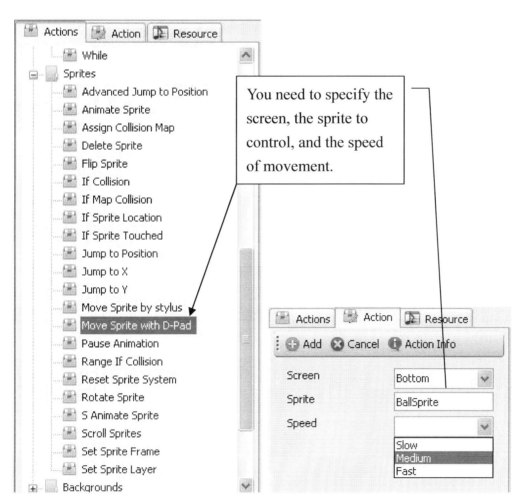

You need to specify the screen, the sprite to control, and the speed of movement.

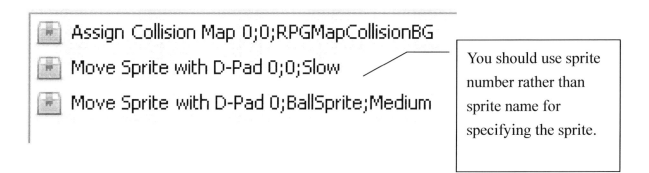

Assign Collision Map 0;0;RPGMapCollisionBG

Move Sprite with D-Pad 0;0;Slow

Move Sprite with D-Pad 0;BallSprite;Medium

You should use sprite number rather than sprite name for specifying the sprite.

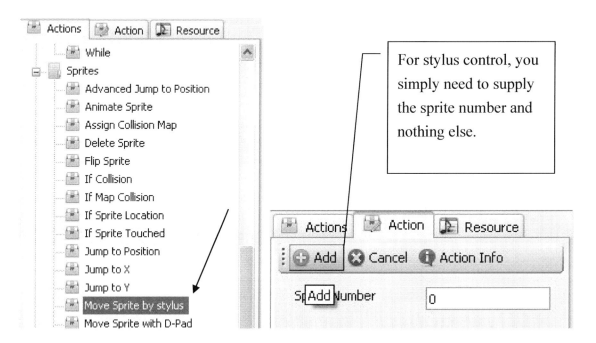

For stylus control, you simply need to supply the sprite number and nothing else.

If you want to use the stylus to move the camera view, this is what you should do:

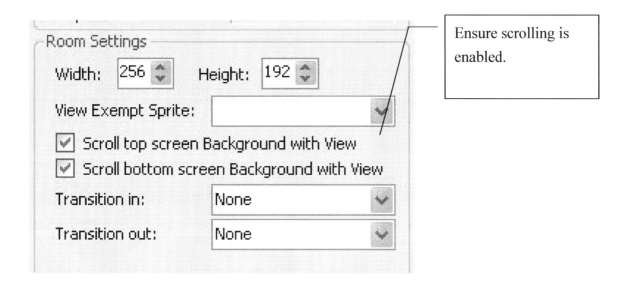

Ensure scrolling is enabled.

Use the set view position action.

The X and Y position should be associated with the stylus's X and Y position.

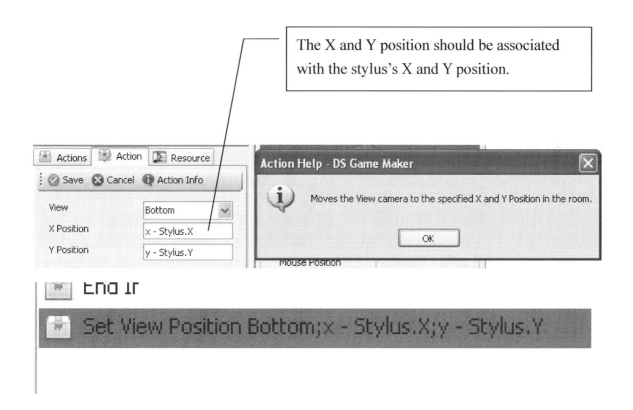

Stylus.X is the X position of the stylus. Stylus.Y is the Y position of the stylus. It is constantly updated by the system.

To use the stylus to "click" on a sprite, you need an action to detect the "clicking". Detection must be specified on a per sprite basis by hand. This is what you should use:

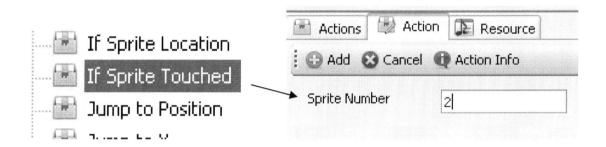

You may also ask the sprite to follow the movement of your stylus. This can be done via the follow stylus action.

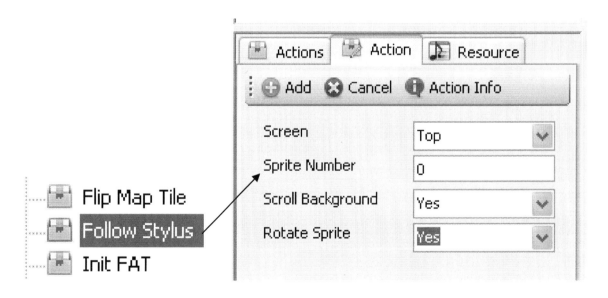

What are the other means of "moving" a sprite?

As said before you can have a sprite moved to a position but there will be no movement action involved.

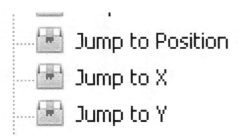

An alternative is to use the advanced jumping action. It allows movement, by a certain amount, to a RELATIVE position of the current position of the SAME SPRITE.

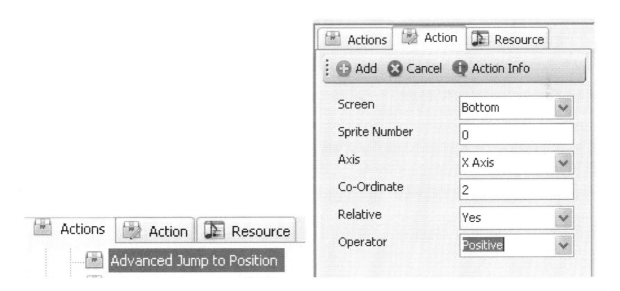

How does sprite animation work? What other actions can I

use to manipulate sprites?

To prepare an animated sprite, you need to lay out all the frames one after another VERTICALLY and SEQUENTIALLY in a single sprite file. There shouldn't be any gaps between frames. And all frames should have the same size. The transparent background must be kept as bright pink as previously mentioned.

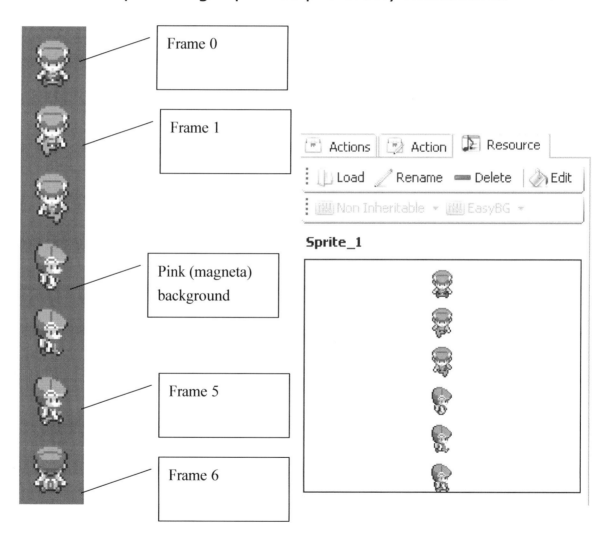

You use these actions to start and stop animation at runtime.

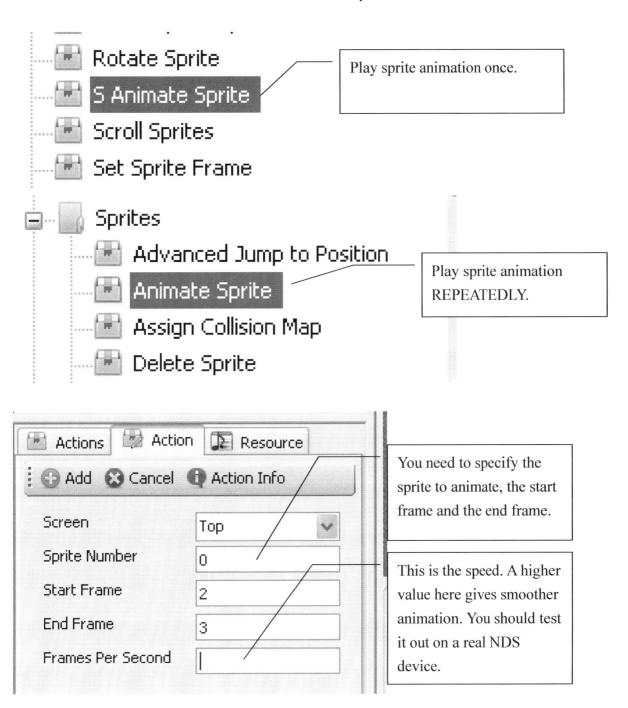

Rotate Sprite

S Animate Sprite — Play sprite animation once.

Scroll Sprites

Set Sprite Frame

Sprites

Advanced Jump to Position

Animate Sprite — Play sprite animation REPEATEDLY.

Assign Collision Map

Delete Sprite

Actions | Action | Resource

Add | Cancel | Action Info

Screen	Top
Sprite Number	0
Start Frame	2
End Frame	3
Frames Per Second	

You need to specify the sprite to animate, the start frame and the end frame.

This is the speed. A higher value here gives smoother animation. You should test it out on a real NDS device.

You may pause the animation as needed. All you need is to specify the sprite to pause.

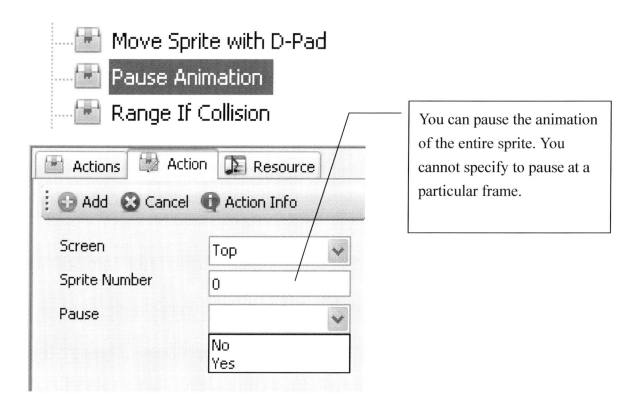

You can pause the animation of the entire sprite. You cannot specify to pause at a particular frame.

You may set the current frame to display as needed. All you need is to specify the sprite and the desired frame number.

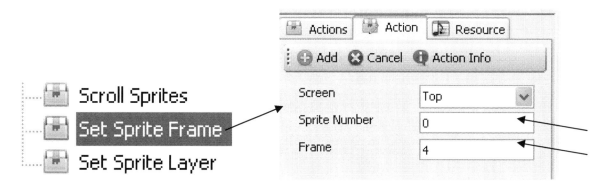

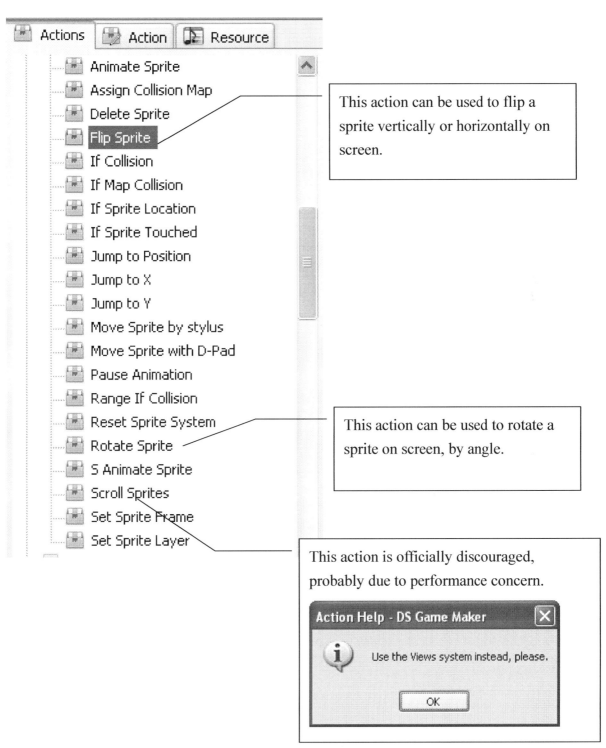

Actions | Action | Resource

- Animate Sprite
- Assign Collision Map
- Delete Sprite
- **Flip Sprite**
- If Collision
- If Map Collision
- If Sprite Location
- If Sprite Touched
- Jump to Position
- Jump to X
- Jump to Y
- Move Sprite by stylus
- Move Sprite with D-Pad
- Pause Animation
- Range If Collision
- Reset Sprite System
- Rotate Sprite
- S Animate Sprite
- Scroll Sprites
- Set Sprite Frame
- Set Sprite Layer

This action can be used to flip a sprite vertically or horizontally on screen.

This action can be used to rotate a sprite on screen, by angle.

This action is officially discouraged, probably due to performance concern.

Action Help - DS Game Maker

ⓘ Use the Views system instead, please.

OK

How do I implement multi-background layer scrolling?

When you have different background elements at different layers, you can scroll them on a per-layer basis without moving the camera view, via the scroll background action. You implement scrolling this way on a layer-by-layer basis.

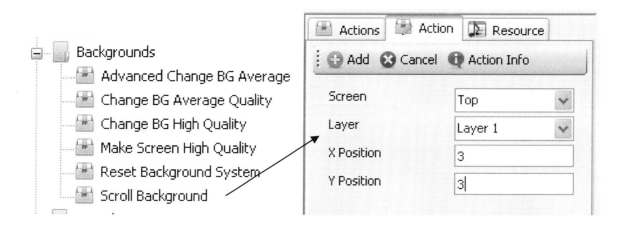

Do keep in mind, scrolling large background elements can be resource consuming. You should test out the actual performance on a real NDS.

What is a loop and how to implement it? What about the do

just once action?

It is believed that the term loop came from the circular looping motion that occurs along flowcharting.

You use a loop to repeat the same action a given number of times or until a condition is met. For the former, you use the LOOP action. For the later, you use the WHILE action.

With LOOP, you specify a variable to act as a counter. The loop repeats as the counter is incremented, until the pre-specified target end value is reached. The action does not create the variable for you so you must declare it separately yourself.

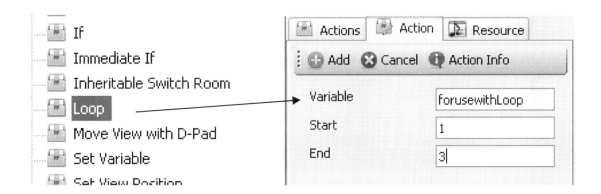

Actions you place between LOOP and END LOOP will be repeated accordingly.

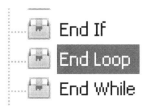

WHILE works differently. There is no counter. The loop is going to repeat as long as a condition is maintained. You define the condition and you will be responsible for any logical error of the condition… If you define an improper condition the loop will either go on forever or will never start…

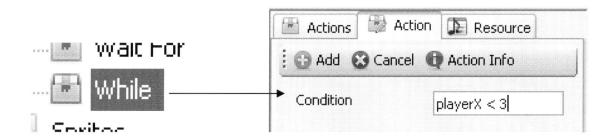

Don't forget to have a matching END WHILE or compilation will fail!

The best thing to do to learn looping is to setup a simple test. Refer to the following example, you use a loop to increment the value of a variable known as displayCount, then you display the result after the loop is completed.

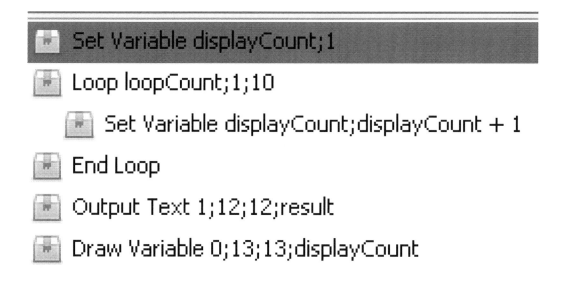

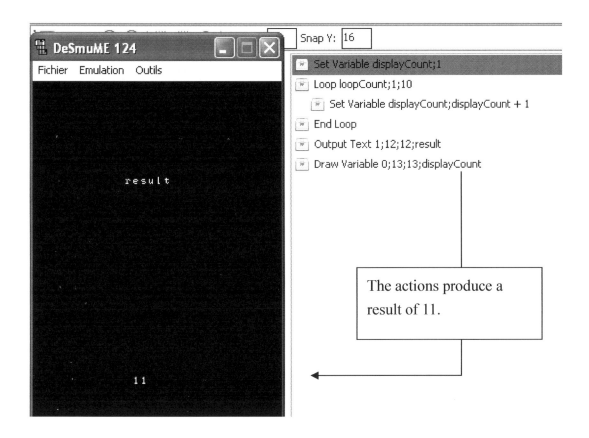

The actions produce a result of 11.

If within the loop you want to include actions that will be performed only once regardless of how the loop is going to repeat, you use the DO JUST ONCE action inside the loop.

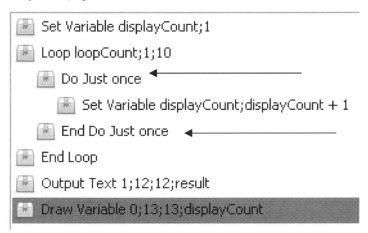

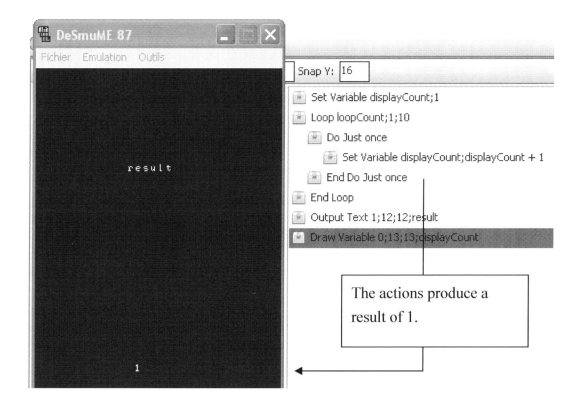

The actions produce a result of 1.

Collision detection – how does it work?

If you are detecting collisions between sprites, use the IF COLLISION action. You need to specify the sprites to be monitored for collision. In other words, collision detection is on a per-pair basis.

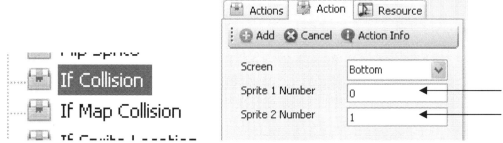

If you want to detect collision between a sprite and the background fixtures (such as the wall, the table...etc), you will need to use a collision map.

We will deal with collision map in depth in volume 2 of this title. For now you need to know the basic concepts – you come up with a background map, and that all passages are to be made transparent (pink). You assign this map (you associate this map with a sprite) and then detect map collision accordingly. Coming up with a proper collision map is a rather advanced technique.

For the latest content update, please visit:

http://www.HobbyPRESS.net/

Please email your questions and comments to

editor@HobbyPRESS.net.

2259215R00053

Printed in Great Britain
by Amazon.co.uk, Ltd.,
Marston Gate.